T0271063

TRADING AS A BUSINESS

The Wiley Trading series features books by traders who have survived the market's ever changing temperament and have prospered–some by reinventing systems, others by getting back to basics. Whether a novice trader, professional or somewhere in-between, these books will provide the advice and strategies needed to prosper today and well into the future. For more on this series, visit our Web site at www.WileyTrading.com.

Founded in 1807, John Wiley & Sons is the oldest independent publishing company in the United States. With offices in North America, Europe, Australia and Asia, Wiley is globally committed to developing and marketing print and electronic products and services for our customers' professional and personal knowledge and understanding.

TRADING AS A BUSINESS

The Methods and Rules I've Used to Beat
the Markets for 40 Years

Dick Diamond

WILEY

Library of Congress Cataloging-in-Publication Data:
Diamond, Dick (Stockbroker)
Trading as a business : the methods and rules I've used to beat the markets for 40 years / Dick Diamond.
    pages cm. —(Wiley trading series)
  Includes index.
  ISBN: 978-1-118-47298-9 (paperback)
  1. Investment analysis. 2. Speculation. 3. Investments. 4. Portfolio management. 5. Stockbrokers. I. Title.
  HG4529.D497 2015
  332.64–dc23
                                                                                               2014032268

Printed in the United States of America

10 9 8 7 6 5 4 3 2 1

CONTENTS

In 1979, I was sitting between two traders at a specialty brokerage firm. The one on my left was on the phone all day, working his contacts to get preopening shares in initial public offerings, which he would jettison at a profit shortly after the deals. He solicited opinions from friends to figure out hot stocks to ride. He was always long, never short. The guy on my right was a plunger who would identify markets that were extended and then bet huge wads on a reversal. I was there when a reversal didn't come, and he was gone.

Sitting across the room was a loner who quietly worked his system. The friend to my left suggested I meet him, so I did. I asked him what he was doing. He said he traded options, and I could sit and watch if I wanted. His name was Dick Diamond.

Most of the traders in the room were chatty, but Dick was quiet. Mostly, he just watched the screen and updated his indicators. Then every now and then he would sit up straight and become hyperalert. Then—bam—he would call in a trade. (There were no electronic trading platforms back then.) He would stay on edge for a period of time, maybe an hour, and then call to close the trade. Then he relaxed again.

When I pressed him about what he was doing, he would talk about waiting for the right "setups," acting swiftly and getting out while momentum was still in his favor, an absolute must when trading options. He seemed more disciplined than other traders. He wasn't trying to win a war; he was in a bunker, taking the occasional shot when his odds of a hit were 80/20. He never changed his tactics, never asked other people their opinions, and never bet big. Incredibly, unlike almost everyone else, he was also making a very good living, every single month.

I liked Dick right away because he was a pure technician. He never acted on news; he didn't care about valuation; he didn't try to solicit inside information; he didn't factor in what the economy was doing, or the president, or the Fed. He just waited for the market to signal the start of a volatile move; then he grabbed a piece of it, time and again. We struck up a friendship that's still ongoing.

In the mid-1980s, Dick and I talked about teaching his method. Subscribers were always asking me about where they could learn trading, and he was ready to show a few people how he did it. So for several years, he taught would-be traders, usually about four at a time, in his Long Island home. They would sit with him for a week as he showed them exactly what he did all day. Despite being shown the ropes, most students, for psychological and other reasons, never became as successful as he is. But every now and then he would report on one who "got it" and was doing well.

In the 2000s, after Dick moved to Florida, he set up seminars that would accommodate 20 or more people. Dick was trading futures by then, but he never changed his entry and exit methods. He and his partners, Roberto Hernandez and Brad Marcus, kept to the format of allowing prospective traders to learn what he was doing, in real time, for a week. Often, he would get dumb questions such as, "When you get stopped out, why don't you just reverse your position?" Dick's usual answer was, "That's not what I do." Secretly, he was thinking, "If you want to lose money on some random idea, go ahead." But, occasionally, an attendee would adopt his method and start winning more than losing.

In the 1990s, I started bugging Dick about writing a book. I said, "Lots of trading books are about making killings and getting killed. Yours will be about chopping it out every day, not for a thrill but as a business. It will be a first." His wife took up the cause.

Many years went by, and no book. Dick is not a writer; he's a trader. After a false start or two, my firm put Dick together with seasoned editor Kevin Commins, with whom we had worked on several projects. Soon the trading book began to take shape.

And here it is!

If you're looking for colorful "war stories," you won't get any. But if you read this book, you will know—as closely as you can absent mathematical codification—just what Dick has been doing all these years.

Dick's approach is so conservative that he's still trading at an age when most people are retired. And he still doesn't have a boss or employees. For most people, trading produces sleepless nights. For him, it produces steady income at retirement age. What a difference! Incredibly, this is absolutely *not* what most traders want. Consciously or unconsciously, they want big scores. That's one reason they end up losing.

Anybody *can* adopt Dick's method. Whether you *do* is another question. But it's all here, and it's very clear.

ROBERT PRECHTER
September 2014

I've been around the trading game for over 40 years. I've seen a lot of traders come and go. But while it's a tough and unforgiving game, it is possible to make a great living from trading. The keys, as I discuss throughout this book, are emotional discipline and risk control.

I've organized this book, *Trading as a Business,* in much the same way that I teach attendees at my seminar. I recount a little bit about my own history as a trader. I discuss the principles that I use to guide my trading and explain the technical indicators that I use. Finally, I reveal my four trading templates and provide dozens of examples of how I use the templates to place trades.

I would suggest reading the entire book from beginning to end and then returning to Chapter 2, "Emotional Discipline"; Chapter 3, "Principles of Successful Trading"; and Chapters 5 through 8, which discuss trading with four different templates. After you've mastered the material, I suggest you set up the trading templates on your computer and begin analyzing the markets every day using the templates. Just as I do in Chapters 5 through 8, you should try to identify 80/20 trades (trades that will produce a profit four out of five times).

I have taught many traders, and I certainly understand that readers will come to this book with different levels of trading experience and expertise in technical analysis. Many of my most successful students adapted parts of my methods to their preexisting approach and evolved into better traders. Roberto Hernandez, a former student who now teaches with me, uses his own trading template, which incorporates some indicators that I do not use at all. If you're going to modify the templates or use your own template, I would suggest a few things. First, and most importantly, do not rely on a single indicator or even two indicators. The markets are too complex to be reducible to a single indicator at all times. I advocate using three to five indicators in a template and waiting until all the indicators align before putting on a trade. Second, make sure that your template is effective in identifying 80/20 trades. From my experience, it's tough to maintain emotional discipline when your template is wrong almost as much as it is right. Finally, read and reread the chapters on trading principles and make them part of your trading DNA. Trade small, use tight stops, and cultivate emotional discipline.

While it's fine to modify my templates or create your own templates, I believe the majority of traders will be better off using the templates in the book. They are the templates I use in my own trading; I know they work.

As I discuss in the chapter on emotional discipline, it's essential that you feel confident in your trading strategies and your trading rules. A trader without confidence will have a hard time pulling the trigger and will constantly second-guess his/her system and rules. A trader with confidence will consistently follow his/her trading signals, will adhere to his/her trading rules, and will accept with equanimity the occasional loss. Remember, as long as you followed your signals and followed your rules, you made a good trade—regardless of whether it produced a profit or loss.

My goal in this book is to give you all the tools you need to trade successfully and to trade with confidence. If you study the material here and work hard to implement the strategies and rules in the market, there's no reason you can't become a consistently profitable trader.

ACKNOWLEDGMENTS

I would like to thank several people who helped me on my path as a teacher of trading and assisted me in the preparation of this book.

First and foremost, I want to thank my wife, Sharie, for giving me motivation, support, and encouragement. Without her, I don't know if I ever would have finished the book.

In many ways, this book is an outgrowth of my trading seminars. I would like to thank Brad Marcus, who got me into teaching in a classroom setting. After I moved to Florida many years ago, I began to take in one or two students for a week. Brad was one of those students. He loved his week with me and proposed that we start a business in which I would teach a group of students for a week three or four times a year. Brad was terrific at organization and he was instrumental in making the business successful.

Bob Prechter has been a close friend and business partner for many years. Bob appealed to me to begin teaching people to trade. For a long time I said no. Finally, we were on vacation together with our families and I told Bob I would try it and see how it worked out. Well, when Bob mentioned that I was providing trading sessions in one of his columns, the phone rang off the hook. Right off the bat, it was a huge success.

Steve Sweet, a partner in Zaner Group, has been very helpful in assisting students with setting up trading accounts and placing trades. I deeply appreciate his presence at our trading seminars in recent years.

Kelly Clement of MetaStock has also been very helpful at seminars, showing students how to create trading templates on their computers using MetaStock. I've used a number of trading software packages over the years, and I consider MetaStock to be the best.

After Brad could no longer participate in the seminars due to other commitments, I began working with Roberto Hernandez. I met Roberto when he attended one of my seminars in 2003. I could tell right away that he was a very bright and very committed trader. He adapted my approach and developed his own unique template. Unlike me, Roberto is a long-term trader. Attendees at our seminars appreciate the perspective and strategies that Roberto brings and how his approach differs from mine, while at the same time conforming to the trading principles I teach.

Finally, I would like to thank the many traders from around the world who have attended my seminars over the years. I enjoyed teaching each and every one of you. I hope this book reinforces what you've learned and helps you to trade more successfully.

CHAPTER 1

My Life as a Trader

I became a full-time trader in 1965. Next to marrying my wife, it was the best decision I ever made. Through trading, I've enjoyed freedom, independence, and prosperity. I have no boss to keep happy; no employees to manage; and no customers to satisfy. Trading has given me a great life.

I work hard, but it's on my own terms. I monitor the U.S. stock market during public trading hours between 9:30 and 4:00, paying particular attention to the morning time period and the hour or so before the close when good trades are most likely to materialize. My after-market analysis takes only about 15 minutes. The rest of my time is my own.

In recent years, I've had the pleasure of teaching my trading approach in classes organized by Elliott Wave International, a company founded by my good friend Robert Prechter. For four days, I talk about trading principles and strategies and conduct live trading. Preparing for the classes and then explaining how I trade to a roomful of people is a great experience. Putting my trading rules and strategies down on slides and presenting to a group of people reinforces to me the ingredients to successful trading. Teaching about trading has made me a better trader.

I get enormous satisfaction when months or even years later an attendee tells me I helped him/her to become a successful trader. I know for a fact that trading can be taught. But not everyone is willing to put in the time and effort necessary to succeed in this business. People often look for easy answers, and, of course, there are too many charlatans in the industry promoting get-rich-quick trading services to the gullible. The truth is there is no substitute for hard work. When someone takes what I taught, works at it and makes it his/her own, and then consistently applies it in the market, I'm thrilled.

With this book, I hope to share my knowledge and experiences about trading with a wider audience and, in so doing, provide aspiring traders with a path to success.

I hold nothing back here. The techniques and principles in this book are the very same techniques and principles that I use every day in the market. Utilizing this approach, I've been able to make a nice living for many years. I'm confident that anyone who diligently and faithfully applies the ideas in this book will develop into a consistently profitable trader.

First a little bit about my background.

I received an undergraduate degree from the Wharton School of Finance and an MBA from the University of Michigan. While the degrees may seem important, I didn't learn anything in college that helped with trading. My father owned seats on both the New York Stock Exchange (NYSE) and the American Stock Exchange (AMEX). He focused on the NYSE seat and rarely used the AMEX seat. Following a stint in the Marines in 1960, I used his AMEX seat and began trading on the AMEX floor.

My job was to fill customer orders on the floor. Once I understood what I was doing, I found the work to be mind-numbingly dull. I pestered my father to allow me to trade my own account. I was young and aggressive. I thought I had a feel for how stocks moved and was sure I could make a lot of money trading AMEX stocks. Finally, in 1965, I got my shot.

The truth is I didn't know much about trading, although I didn't realize it at the time. I made progressively more money from 1965 to 1968. My good fortune had less to do with skill and more to do with the competitive advantages I enjoyed and overall market conditions. Trading from the floor of the AMEX allowed me to trade faster and with lower commissions than most other investors. And most important, we were in the midst of a strong bull market phase.

At the time, there were a lot of cheap stocks selling on the AMEX. My strategy—if you want to call it that—was to watch the order flow, and when a big buy order came in for one of these cheap stocks, I would jump in and take a position. I would usually get out later in the day or sometimes the following day. I would make fractions on many of the trades: one-eighth to maybe three-eighths of a point. The strategy generally worked as long as the market remained in a bull phase. Sometimes a stock would go its own way; the low-priced stocks I favored had a weak correlation to the overall market. But, even so, I was doing well.

Probably as a result of my early success, I got into some bad habits. I started holding on to losers for too long, thinking they would eventually rally. Most of the time, they did. Then one time, they didn't. It was a disaster.

In late 1968, I had positions in 15 different stocks. I held maybe 15,000 or 20,000 shares. They were all the kind of low-priced, go-go stocks that the AMEX was pushing at the time. Many of the companies no longer exist today. We went on a family vacation and I decided to let the positions ride. I didn't have stops in place and I wasn't even committed to checking on the positions while I was away. It was probably the craziest thing I ever did as a trader. You can probably guess what happened. The stock market tanked. Two weeks later, I had lost 70 percent of my trading capital.

I was at a crossroads. I sat down with my wife and discussed the situation. We decided that either I was going to do this right or I was going to find another career. We joked that if trading didn't work out, I was going to do oil changes. What pulled me through was my motivation. I never gave up the goal of becoming a successful trader. I was determined to give it my best shot.

Slowly, I changed my approach. I talked to successful traders and discovered that many of them used technical analysis. I read whatever books I could find on technical analysis at my local library and elsewhere. I subscribed to a weekly charting service and updated the charts by hand every day until the next week's charts arrived. I began to get a feel for market direction. I started shorting stocks when my analysis indicated stocks were headed lower, which is something I had never done before. Eventually, I became an acceptable short-term trader.

I also changed the stocks I traded. Instead of trading low-priced, highly volatile, "flier" stocks, I focused on large-cap stocks that tracked the overall market much more closely. Finally, I took small positions and got out quickly. As a result, my risk control improved dramatically.

They say history doesn't repeat, but it rhymes. The bull market of the 1960s was very similar in tone and substance to the bull market in the 1990s. In the 1960s, we had the so-called "nifty fifty" that drove the market higher and higher. In the 1990s, newly formed Internet companies created massive interest in the market. A lot of traders made money by betting on the long side of the market in both decades. When everything is going up, it's not hard to make money.

Many of you probably remember that the Internet-fueled bull market ended with a resounding thud in 2001. From January 14, 2000, to October 9, 2002, the market lost 31.5 percent of its value. Suddenly, many traders who did well in the 1990s weren't doing so great anymore. Markets change, and when traders don't change with them, they lose their shirts.

The 1960s were similar. From June 1962 to February 1966, the market rose 86 percent. After a sell-off for eight months in 1966, the market took off again, rising 32 percent from October 1966 to December 1968. Then, as always happens, everything changed. From November 1968 to May 1970, the market fell 36 percent. That was my Pearl Harbor, so to speak. I learned my lesson and was prepared for the next bear market.

From 1973 to 1975, the Dow lost 45 percent of its value. By this time, I was comfortable shorting stocks and keeping my bets small. I didn't get attached to losers hoping they would come back. I had begun to learn one of the most important components to successful trading: emotional control.

Flexibility is important in trading, just as it is in life. It's good to take advantage of new opportunities that arise. In 1975, the Chicago Board Options Exchange introduced options on stocks. After studying how options worked, I decided to incorporate them in my trading. At that time, they gave me leverage that I found useful for my short-term, low-risk trading strategies. Nowadays, I primarily use options when I sense a big move is afoot.

The Chicago Mercantile Exchange (CME) introduced futures on the Standard & Poor's (S&P) index in 1980. Then in 1997, the CME began trading E-mini futures, which were a scaled-down version of the S&P futures contract. Trading volume on the E-minis soared, and they quickly became my preferred day-trading vehicle. I can get in and out of the E-minis quickly and efficiently, and I can utilize the margin available on the E-minis without any complication. They are a great tool for day trading.

The advent of personal computers, electronic trading, and reduced commissions significantly leveled the playing field for independent traders in the 1990s—myself included. With a mouse click you're in or out of a trade. Compare that to the old days of calling in an order on the telephone. Despite this amazing advancement in the speed of execution, I hear people complain that big institutional traders may be able to execute trades a microsecond faster than an independent trader. Speaking for myself, this is not a problem. I get excellent fills on my trades. And I'm not trading huge size.

I don't see a dramatic difference between the price movements in the market today and when I first started in the business. Support and resistance, momentum, divergence, cycles, chart patterns—they all function in much the same way now as they did in the 1960s. No one indicator is perfect. But combining indicators intelligently allows you to read the market and identify situations where the odds are heavily in your favor. Despite what you might read elsewhere about how computers have ruined the stock market, there is an opportunity for independent traders.

Market conditions always evolve. After the Internet bubble, the market veered sideways to slightly down until 2003. We had a weak bull market from 2003 to 2007. Then from 2007 to 2009, we experienced the worst bear market since the 1930s. Starting in early 2009, the market rallied, making up all of the gains lost in the previous bear market. As I write this, the bull market continues, although it sometimes appears it is losing steam and a correction—or new market phase—may be imminent.

Although I'm primarily a day trader, I try to understand big-picture market conditions. I'm always aware of the major and secondary trends. That said, I keep my bias as slight as possible going into any given trading day. A bias is just that: a sense that the market is more likely to trend in a particular direction on a particular day, but it is not an ironclad opinion. Sometimes my bias is wrong. And sometimes things happen outside the market that completely change the complexion of the day. I stay flexible and adjust my analysis in real time in response to market action.

I don't pay too much attention to the opinions of other traders or market analysts. I do my own homework, do my own real-time analysis, and do my own trading. I think it's important to be self-reliant in this business. Yes, you can learn from other traders. But you have to integrate what you learn into your own process of analyzing the market, identifying good trades, and executing those trades. If you want to succeed in this business, you have to learn how to trade for yourself—no one else can do it for you.

After my big loss in 1969, the changes I made to my trading enabled me to adjust to the changing market climates over the next five decades. I go long or short in response to opportunities. I don't force trades. I wait for high-probability trades. And I stay flexible, which has allowed me to make money even when my long-term and medium-term analysis was off the mark.

The biggest change I've made from when I started trading in the 1960s is my attitude toward risk. As I mentioned, when I first started trading, I went after the market like a tiger stalking its prey. No more. I now consider myself a "scaredy-cat." I respect the market: It will go where it goes, and I believe there's no one in the world who can consistently predict the market's direction. I have my templates for identifying high-probability trades. But if the trades don't work out quickly, I'm out. And when they do go in my direction, I grab my profits.

I marvel at some of the big hedge-fund operators I read about in the financial press who make huge bets on one particular idea. Sometimes they hit the jackpot. I recall one example where a trader foresaw the housing crash and shorted mortgage-backed securities and other housing-related instruments. I gather he made hundreds of millions for his fund. I understood his subsequent bets—long gold and short the Chinese stock market—were far less successful. I don't mean to diminish this individual. Obviously, this approach works for some people. It's just not the way I operate.

■ Trading as a Business

I look at trading as a long-term, money-making business. I'm not looking for the big score or even a series of big scores. I want to stay around for the long haul. My first priority is to avoid losing money. My second priority is to capitalize on the market's short-term swings to eke out consistent profits. Sure, I have losing days. But I rarely have a losing week. And I haven't had a losing month in years.

The key to what I do is to wait for high-probability situations—what I call 80/20 trades. I define my 80/20 setups, patiently wait for them to develop, and then act decisively. I anticipate trades. And once the setup materializes, I pull the trigger. I don't force the issue, but I don't overanalyze either. Some days, I make no trades at all; other days, I make four or five trades. I take what the market gives me.

The mind-set I try to cultivate through all this is quiet confidence. Without confidence, it's very difficult to trade. To me, quiet confidence is a function of emotional control, faith in my methods, and following my trading rules. I understand and accept that some trades will be losers. I do not accept violating my trading rules.

I will go into all these matters in more depth in later chapters. For now, I want to underscore that with the proper trading principles and technical analysis tools, you can learn how to consistently make money in up and down markets. You can make trading your business.

Trading has many advantages over other businesses you might contemplate starting, for example:

- You choose what you want to trade, when to trade it, and in any amount you wish.

- You have no customers to keep happy.

- You have no employees to keep happy.

- You have no product to make, to advertise, or to sell.

- You have nothing to store.

- You have no invoices to send out, no accounts payable, no accounts receivables, and no bad checks.

- Buyers and sellers are immediately available when you want to transact a trade.

- You alone are responsible for the success of your business.

- You can scale up or scale down the business at your discretion.

- You can trade from anywhere.

In the pages that follow, I discuss trading principles, rules, and 80/20 trades. I explain the indicators I use, how I set up my computer screen, and the precise alignment of indicators I look for to put on a trade. I discuss money management, markets to trade, and how I use options to complement my core strategies. Most important, I emphasize emotional control. If you let emotions intrude on your trading decisions, there's no way you can succeed at this game.

I understand that it's not possible for everyone to day trade. You may have a full-time job and can't trade during the day as I do. Or you may not want to look at a computer screen throughout the day. That's fine. You can adjust my indicators to longer time frames and set slightly larger stop-loss levels and profit targets. You can do your analysis at night and place your orders prior to the market open.

Many traders who come to my classes already have developed a method for analyzing the market and identifying trades. Sometimes they just need to learn more about trading principles or tactics to become successful. For example, while I don't use Elliott Wave, I've known many traders who do, and they have told me that my classes helped them to become better traders.

While I trade the E-mini futures, you may want to trade individual stocks, exchange-traded funds, commodities, or currencies. My setups work in all markets. Whatever you trade, however, make sure there is sufficient liquidity to get in and out of the market efficiently. Later in the book, I will discuss how I use options. Options can enhance your trading, but there are some popular options strategies that are best to avoid.

My conviction is that with proper knowledge, effort, and discipline, most people attracted to trading can become successful. I hope this book illuminates the path to success in trading. The rest is up to you.

CHAPTER 2

Emotional Discipline

The centerpiece of my trading is the identification and proper execution of what I call 80/20 trades. I define 80/20 trades as setups that historically have been profitable about 80 percent of the time. I don't trade 60/40 situations. And I don't trade situations where I have a feeling that market is going to go in a particular direction if my feeling is not corroborated by one of my 80/20 setups.

I spent years experimenting with various technical indicators and combining them in different ways to create the best possible trading setups. Some of the technical indicators I use are fairly common, such as moving average convergence-divergence (MACD) or stochastics. Others are a little more esoteric, such as the Walter Bressert indicator and the Rahul Mohindar oscillator (RMO). I use them because they work in trading. I'm a pragmatist, not a theoretician.

I look for all my indicators on any particular template to be pointing in the same direction before putting on a trade. That means waiting patiently for the right situation to emerge and passing up many situations that do not completely match my criteria. It's perfectly acceptable to miss a trade. There will always be new opportunities. What you don't want to do is force the action and get into 60/40 trades out of greed, boredom, or some other emotional motivation. You must avoid 60/40 trades at all costs!

If you want to exactly replicate my trading screen, you'll need to subscribe to the MetaStock service. I've used a few other software programs in my career, but, in my opinion, MetaStock is the best. Of course, you may like another software system and choose to continue with it. You should know, however, that while most of my indicators are on other services, only MetaStock has the Bressert and

RMO indicators. In the appendix, I've included a section written by Kelly Clement of MetaStock that describes how to set up my templates via MetaStock.

Once you have the templates on your computer, I suggest monitoring how they respond in real markets for at least four weeks. It's one thing for me to assert that these setups work. It's another thing—and much more important—for you to be convinced that you can make the setups work for you.

You may want to paper trade for a period of time. You can gain experience and the feel of putting on trades, placing stops, moving stops, and exiting trades. Monitor your results closely, and when you feel you've reached a good level of proficiency and your results are satisfactory, you can begin trading with real money.

You always want to use stops—even in paper trading. Put a stop in with your initial order and move the stop in the direction of the trade as the trade becomes profitable. That's what I do. Never take for granted risk control, and don't let a profit turn into a loss. Markets can change in an instant, and you should always protect your position.

I trade on two-minute charts. I usually set my initial stop two ticks away from entry price. As the price moves in my favor, I'll push the stop higher or lower to protect my position. If the market doesn't move fast enough, I may liquidate the trade before it hits my protective stop. It's better to break even than take a two-tick loss. My initial goal is not to lose money.

When I enter an 80/20 trade on a two-minute chart, I expect the market will move quickly in the direction of the trade. I'm looking for a free ride. If the ride doesn't come quickly, I'll get out.

My templates work on longer time frames, too. You may not be able to monitor the market throughout the day, or you may simply prefer to trade on a different time frame. That's fine. You can adjust the bars to 30, 60, 120 minutes—whatever time frame you prefer. As you move out to a longer time frame, remember two things: (1) you'll need to set wider stops, perhaps six to eight ticks, and (2) you'll need to hold on to your trades for a longer period of time.

Apart from any time frame adjustment, I would advise sticking with the settings I use on the indicators and templates. If you want to tweak an indicator to see how it responds to a different setting, that's OK. It may give you some valuable insights. However, you don't want to constantly change the settings. The worst thing you can do is to change the settings following every trade that doesn't work.

About one in five or six 80/20 trades identified by my templates doesn't work out. That's acceptable because if you execute the templates consistently, you will make money. The templates enable you to identify situations where the percentages are in our favor and execute trades in a disciplined and consistent manner. If you keep changing your indicators, you'll undermine your confidence, and without confidence it's difficult to trade.

Everything in trading is connected: trade setups, money management, and emotional discipline. To be profitable, you need both high-percentage trade setups and good money management tactics. And to execute 80/20 trades and adhere to sound money management principles, you need to be emotionally disciplined. All three elements are required to be a successful trader.

■ Why Traders Fail

The most important component to successful trading can be described in two words: emotional discipline. You must develop the ability to patiently wait for a tradable situation to develop, and then, when it's in front of you, execute the trade. It sounds simple, but, believe me, the lack of emotional discipline is the number one reason that traders fail.

Some traders tend to force trades when the odds are not in their favor. Others have difficulty pulling the trigger when a good trade presents itself. On the back end, some traders hold on to trades too long. As a result, losses frequently become bigger and profits frequently become smaller. These are all problems of emotional discipline.

As I transformed myself from a losing trader to a winning trader, it became apparent to me that emotional discipline was my key to success. Sure, I had developed a process for analyzing the market and identifying good trades, and that was a big challenge. But emotional discipline proved to be a much more difficult skill to master.

Regardless of whether you're a short-term trader like me or a long-term trend trader, emotional discipline is central to success. One of the most famous long-term trend traders of all time is Richard Dennis. Like me, he believes the emotional and psychological factors are more important than market analysis in determining success or failure.

"The key is consistency and discipline," Dennis said in the book *Market Wizards*. "Almost anybody can make up a list of rules that are 80% as good as we taught. What they can't do is give people confidence to stick to those even when things are going bad."

Dennis believed trading could be taught. As an experiment, he recruited 23 traders from a large pool of applicants and taught them a trend-following strategy, money management techniques, and gave them capital to trade. While some of them failed, a significant number were highly profitable. The experience reinforced Dennis' conviction that discipline is the most important component of trading. The traders who most closely followed the system and money management rules were the most successful.

The trading system that Richard Dennis taught has been public knowledge for years. Similarly, Warren Buffett's method for buying and selling stocks is well known. In addition, Buffett's stock holdings are fully disclosed and easily available. Yet very few investors and very few traders come anywhere near the performance of Dennis and Buffett.

Sometimes it strikes me that trading is similar to weight loss. Knowledge is not the problem. Everyone knows that to lose weight you need to burn more calories than you consume. If you eat the right foods in the right amounts and exercise consistently, you'll lose weight. It's as simple as that. Yet there are hundreds of books on dieting and an entire industry devoted to helping people lose weight. Just as in trading, in weight loss the critical factor is emotional discipline. You have to do the right thing consistently, even if it feels uncomfortable.

For a complete understanding of the topic, I recommend a book entitled *Emotional Discipline* by Charles Manz (Berrett-Koehler, 2003). In essence, the book talks about a process to identify, understand, and reframe your emotions. I think the process can be a great help to traders who have trouble trading in an objective, rational, and disciplined manner.

■ Core Position and 80/20 Trades

While I believe emotional discipline is the most important factor in trading success, you also need a method to identify profitable trades and sufficient capital to trade. Later in the book, I provide the templates I use to identify high-probability trades. In regard to capital, determining and adhering to your core position is an absolute necessity to succeed over the long haul.

A core position is the trading size that you can execute in the market without becoming emotional. Sure, you enter into every trade intending it to be a winner. But when a trade doesn't work out, you should be able to exit with a small loss and without any emotional pain. Similarly, when a trade works in your favor, you should be able to grab your profits at the right time. You shouldn't hold on too long out of greed or exit too early out of fear.

My core position is very small relative to my account size. My maximum position is 10 E-minis, which is equivalent to two Standard & Poor's (S&P) futures contracts. I often scale into positions whereby I buy/sell maybe 5 E-minis initially. But even if the initial position is very profitable, I will not exceed my core position of 10 E-minis in building out the trade. I simply don't trade over my core position.

You need to find a position size where you're not overwhelmed with feelings of hope, fear, and greed. If you only have a few thousand dollars to trade, the position might be a few hundred dollars of individual stocks. That's fine. Once you identify and adhere to a core position from which you can trade with emotional discipline, you're on the way to long-term success.

■ The Emotions of Trading

The feeling you want to cultivate in trading is quiet confidence and self-control. When you begin trading, you need to base your confidence on knowledge that you can identify high-probability trades and you can follow the trading rules. You need to trade small. As you gain experience, your confidence will grow. You may be able to increase the size of your core position. *But be careful.* Many traders, after a string of good trades, get cocky and take on too much risk. Trust me—the market is a merciless teacher.

Greed

The object of trading is to make money. However, to make money you have to focus on finding good trades and executing according to your trading rules. If you focus too much on the money, you very well may lose sight of the trading process that generates long-term success.

In its most blatant form, greed leads traders to take too much risk, override their systems, and hold on to losing trades too long. A trader who is thinking about an expensive car or an oceanfront vacation home is setting himself up for big problems. Banish that kind of thinking and imagery from your mind.

Greed can be subtle, too. It can creep into your trading at any point in your career. If you're on a hot streak, you may be tempted to trade too large or stay in trades too long. Or you may start taking lesser trades when you have a feeling about the market direction, even though the feeling is not corroborated by your signals.

Some traders set profit objectives. I think this is a mistake. What are you going to do on the last trading day of the month if you are 10 percent short of your monthly profit target? The natural inclination is to trade more aggressively to hit your target. To do so, you might override your signals and break your rules.

Remember, you can only trade what the market gives you. There will be periods with many trading opportunities and periods when there are few chances to make money. Focus on the market, your signals, and your rules. The money will take care of itself.

Fear

It's very difficult to trade when you're anxious and nervous. Not only is anxiety an uncomfortable feeling, it actually worsens performance. A fearful trader anticipates failure. When you're wracked by fear, it's difficult to objectively interpret market activity and to follow your trading rules. You have trouble assessing opportunities and pulling the trigger. You're prone to paralysis by analysis.

From my personal experiences and knowledge of other traders, fear can have many causes:

- Lack of confidence in your trade selection criteria.

- Lack of confidence in your trading rules.

- Undercapitalization.

- Fear of losing money.

- Fear of failure.

First, it's important to acknowledge that trading is not easy. No one can forecast where markets will go. All you can do is search for tradable situations and execute your trades in a disciplined fashion. Given the challenges of trading, a healthy respect for the markets is certainly warranted. However, you can't let respect grow into fear. You can't let yourself become immobilized.

One of my goals in this book is to provide you with high-probability trade setups and a set of trading rules that have worked for me for many years. You need to study the setups, get the proper indicators on your computer, and monitor the markets until you can consistently identify the 80/20 trades. At the same time, you need to ingrain the rules of trading discussed throughout this book. Once you have mastered both the setups and the rules, you're ready to begin trading. Then, as you execute correctly in live markets, you will develop confidence.

Fear of losing money and having insufficient capital to trade go hand-in-hand. You need to have enough trading capital and then trade in a size that won't lead you to become overly emotional. If you're counting how much money you're winning or losing with every tick, you need to reduce your trading size. You have to trade the market and your indicators, not the money.

Economists who have studied investor behavior have discovered that, for most people, the pain of losing money is greater than the pleasure in making money. They call this loss aversion. For traders, loss aversion can lead to paralysis. You become unwilling to take a trade because there's a possibility of losing money.

As a trader, you need to accept that losses are part of the game. Every trade you make has the potential to be a loser. If you adhere to a sound method and sound trading rules, you will win over time. As long as your trading process is correct, you shouldn't allow yourself to be bothered by losing trades. You just have to keep your losses small.

Fear of failure is similar but slightly different than the fear of losing money. The trader who is afraid of failure typically spends an enormous amount of time and energy on analyzing markets and creating and testing trading systems. This type of trader is afraid that his or her intellectual understanding of the markets will be proven wrong if he actually trades on the basis of his analysis. For this type of trader, the market is more of a fascinating intellectual puzzle than a playing field where money can be made by skillful trading.

There are many intelligent and perceptive people who closely follow the financial markets. Some of them write newsletters and provide analysis on behalf of brokerage firms. Surprisingly, a significant number of these people do not trade on the basis of their own analytical work. To trade and fail would undermine the value of their work—at least in their own minds. Fear of failure keeps them on the sidelines.

Impatience

A trader who tries to make money too quickly by overtrading or who desperately wants to be in the market to feel the excitement of the game is destined to lose in the long run. You have to have the patience to choose your spots. There are days I sit in front of my computer and do not make a trade. Now, it isn't as though I'm doing nothing. I'm monitoring the market and waiting for a tradable situation. If a good situation doesn't materialize, I stay on the sidelines. Patience is a virtue in trading.

Similarly, your long-term goals in trading should be realistic. Banish the thought of getting rich quickly through trading. You should strive to diligently follow your trading rules and trade only high-probability setups. The money will follow. Remember, the turtle wins the race.

■ The Importance of Commitment

Most people do not succeed as traders due to a lack of emotional discipline. While following your trading rules and trading well-defined setups may sound easy enough, the reality is that following these principles in live markets with real money at stake is always challenging. You're going to have successes and you're going to have failures. The most important thing is to always limit your risk and remain consistent in the application of trading rules and the situations you choose to trade.

As with any worthwhile endeavor, commitment is necessary for long-term success in trading. You can't become a profitable trader with a half-hearted effort. You need to fully commit intellectually, financially, and emotionally. Above all else, commit yourself to emotional discipline.

CHAPTER 3

Principles of Successful Trading

A s we've discussed, trading can be a great business. However, the majority of people who trade fail to make money consistently. In this chapter, we'll discuss trading principles that are the foundation of my trading. I urge you to read and reread this section. You must understand and apply these principles in your trading to succeed. I can't stress this enough: **The implementation of these principles in your day-to-day trading will allow you to develop emotional discipline. And only with emotional discipline can you become a successful long-term, independent trader.**

■ Trade within Your Capital

In trading, everyone makes mistakes. Even the best, most experienced traders occasionally misread the market. In addition, you may do everything right on a trade, but something happens out of the blue that causes the market to reverse direction. Either occurrence—a market misread or an out-of-the-blue event—will result in a losing trade. Losing trades are part of the business. They happen to everyone, and they will happen to you. That being the case, you always want to lose small.

To lose small, you must trade small relative to your overall capital. If you have a $20,000 account, you don't want to risk $2,000 on a single trade. It's too much of a hit to take given your overall capital. A small series of $2,000 losses is going to destroy your confidence and likely will cause you to stop trading entirely or take too much risk on an all-or-nothing trade in hopes of recouping your losses. To stay in the market for the long haul, you need to trade small.

I've often seen traders increase the size of their trades following a series of winning trades. Think about the logic of that for a moment. It's axiomatic that losing trades are inevitable. After a series of winning trades, do you think a losing trade or series of losing trades is more or less likely? In my experience, a winning streak is usually followed by a losing period or at least a few losing trades. If you increase the size of your trades, you're likely to give everything back and then some.

Beginning traders often come into the market with unrealistic ambitions. They think they will consistently make money, continually raise the size of their trades as their account grows, and within a short period of time, they'll amass a small fortune. A more realistic goal for a beginning trader is to learn the business while making modest profits and taking small losses. First, you learn to survive. Then you learn to thrive. Yes, you can grow your account and, at some point, increase your size. But you have to go after it like a turtle, not like a Ferrari.

There is another element to trading small. Every trader has a position size that he/she cannot exceed without endangering his or her emotional discipline. I call it my core position. Although I can trade much larger, my core position is 10 E-mini contracts, which is equivalent to two Standard & Poor's (S&P) contracts. This is my maximum position. If I trade larger, I'll begin to lose my emotional discipline.

You need to find a position size that allows you to execute your trades objectively, unemotionally, and consistently. It may be much smaller than what you're currently contemplating. It might be 10 shares of a $100 stock. That's fine. As you get comfortable, you can increase your position size—within reason. The point is that you never want to trade at a size where the emotions of hope, greed, and fear overwhelm your rational mind and objective decision-making process.

The business of trading is all about controlling emotions. You should not fight the market or other traders. You should not fight yourself. You need to keep greed and fear low and discipline high. Hope is a great emotion in other aspects of life, but not in trading. Find your core position and stick with it.

■ Quiet Confidence

Of course, we are emotional creatures and we can't completely strip emotions out of trading. The feeling that I recommend you cultivate is quiet confidence.

Quiet confidence comes from following your trading rules and faithfully executing high-probability trades. It comes from trading within your capital and exercising emotional discipline. And it comes from the knowledge that if you do the right things in trading, good results will follow.

When you have quiet confidence, you are in complete control of your trades.

At a gambling casino, you have less than a 50/50 chance of winning. The odds always favor the house. I've read that a player's odds in most Las Vegas establishments are about 46/54. What that means is that once you've rolled your dice at the craps table, you're committed to a bet where the odds are stacked against you and you can't do a darn thing about it. You never want to do that in trading.

In trading—at least the way I go about it—you never really let go of the dice. You wait for the high-probability trade to materialize. You make the trade. You monitor the position. Depending on market action, you get out of the trade with either a profit or, at worst, a small loss. In a sense, you never really let go of the dice in this type of trading. You remain in control throughout the process.

When you lack confidence, you can't win. The quickest way to lose your confidence is to violate one of your trading rules. It's OK to make an incorrect call on the market. But it is not OK to violate a trading rule. Once you start making excuses for violating your rules, the entire foundation of your trading will crumble and you'll be back to square one.

You are most vulnerable to breaking your rules following a string of good trades. For a period of time in the late 1970s and early 1980s, I found myself doing much better than normal. I attributed my improved results to better trading on my part. Thinking that I had now reached a higher level of trading proficiency, I increased my trading size. I remember getting emotional and little greedy. Then the inevitable happened. The market went against me and I took a big hit. Lesson learned.

If you are making more money than usual, it's probably because the market conditions are creating more trading opportunities, not because you're a better trader. When you're doing well, refocus your energy on following your trading rules and avoid thinking about money. Don't let quiet confidence develop into overconfidence.

Similarly, confidence should not cause you to become too committed to a market view. Market conditions can change several times during an active day. A trader needs to be pliable and adjust his/her viewpoint in concert with changing market conditions. You can't think that you know better than everyone else and you know better than the market. That's not confidence—that's arrogance. And arrogant traders never win.

When you are quietly confident, you can trade without beating yourself up over setbacks or getting too high after successes. Assuming you have a good trading process in place, you should trade the same regardless of your recent results. Don't become more aggressive, and don't become more cautious following success or failure. Don't dwell on the past. Focus on the *now* and the next trade that's in front of you.

■ Sell Too Soon, Not Too Late

I'm an in-and-out trader. I focus on short-term situations where I have an 80 percent chance of winning. On a typical day I make three or four trades. Given my style, it's important for me to grab a quick profit or liquidate a trade if it doesn't move in my favor. I exit quickly.

Good traders don't worry about missing a chunk of a big move. They take their profits without regrets. They know they can always get back into the market. In a sense, they're content with taking a piece of the pie and coming back for seconds.

In trading, everyone agrees that you should cut your losses. However, you sometimes hear or read that you should "let your profits run." The idea is that you wait until the move is exhausted before selling. I don't agree with this tactic at all. Here's why:

It's a rare event for a market to make a move early in the morning and then continue in that direction the entire day. Typically, there are pullbacks or small consolidation points along the way. Sometimes the market reverses, sometimes the trend continues, and sometimes the market transitions into a trading range. The patterns are endless. The trader who had the mind-set of letting his/her profits run is, in essence, hoping for an unusual market structure: a trend day that moves strongly in one direction and never looks back. Those days happen, but they are a rarity.

In most circumstances, if you "let your profits run," you'll end up waiting too long and selling after a protracted pullback. You're likely to give back a good portion of your profits on the trade. Moreover, by overstaying the trade, you may miss out on the next trade. The pullback where you exited may be setting up for another 80/20 trade.

The best time to sell is when the momentum is in your favor. You see the 80/20 trade. You get in. The market moves in your direction, and you have a nice profit on the trade. Take it. Get out and get ready for the next trade. Do this three or four times a day and you'll end up winning most days and nearly every week. That's how a lot of professional traders make a living.

You never want to find yourself wishing or hoping for the market to do something. You want to remain in control of the trade and in control of your emotions. Winners come into a trade for a quick profit. If it doesn't work out, they get out. Losing traders hold on to hope. And if the trade doesn't work for them, their hope usually turns to regret or despair over losing money. That's not a path to long-term trading success.

As you gain experience in the market, you'll get a better sense of market action and the right time to get out. There will be times when you catch a trade just right and the momentum is very strong in your favor. In those cases, you can hold on a little longer than usual. In other cases, where the market doesn't move much at all after putting on a trade, you might elect to get out earlier with maybe a scratch or a small profit.

You always want to control your trade. If you have doubt about a trade, get out of it right away and stay out until the situation becomes clearer to you. You always want to strive for an objective appraisal of the market and unemotional trade execution. Hope, doubt, fear, and greed are enemies of good trading.

Take Personal Responsibility for Your Trading

You alone are responsible for your results in trading. You get to pick how to trade, what to trade, and when to trade. You are the reason you succeed or fail in trading. A sure sign of a bad trader is one who places blame on factors other than himself for his results.

Bad traders can come up with a variety of excuses for a losing trade:

- I got a bad tip.

- The pros went gunning for stops—and they got mine.

- My broker gave me a bad fill.

- My computer crashed.

- The price quotes were delayed.

- I was interrupted or distracted.

- A news event caused the market to reverse.

- And on and on.

Again, losses are inevitable in trading. You need to learn to handle them without getting down on yourself or blaming an external factor. While it's fine to analyze a losing trade to understand what went wrong, don't dwell on it. Don't dwell on winners either. Get back to the market and get ready for the next trade.

I make about 15 trades on the average week. I expect about 12 of them to be profitable. Some will be marginally profitable, and some will be very profitable. The losses on the losing trades will be small. At the end of the week, I'm almost always in the black. That said, I do have losing days. That's acceptable. If I have a losing week (which is very rare), I examine what I've done to see if some bad habits have crept into any aspect of my trading. A bad month is completely unacceptable.

Wait for 80/20 Trades

As I've said, the heart of my approach is to trade high-probability setups, which I define as trades that have an 80 percent chance of winning. I have created templates, which I share in later chapters, to recognize these trades. The key for me is to wait patiently for the high-probability trade to materialize before putting on a trade.

There will be many times when you have a strong feeling that the market is going to move in a particular direction. Maybe the market has broken out from a trading range and looks ready to go higher. Or maybe an up move has run out of steam and the market is turning the other way. These types of situations happen all the time, and it's natural as an observer of market action that you get a sense of the market's next move. However—and I can't emphasize this enough—do not trade on these feelings until they are corroborated by the 80/20 trading template.

I like to say I'm a "sore loser." I do not trade 60/40 situations, and you shouldn't either. At the end of the day, the profit margins are too small to make these trades worthwhile. And when you lose 40 percent of the time, you're more prone to losing streaks, losing days, and losing weeks. Also, when your loss rate is 40 percent, you are more likely to second-guess your signals and have difficulty pulling the trigger.

It's OK to stay on the sidelines when the market is giving you mixed signals. I trade the market by my own set of rules. If the current market action doesn't give me the kind of opportunity I demand, then I don't play.

■ Play Great Defense

A good trader is more focused on controlling risk than maximizing profit. He or she does this by accomplishing the following:

- Controlling emotions so that fear and greed do not undermine the decision-making process
- Getting out of losing trades quickly
- Following the trading rules
- Trading small relative to the size of his/her capital.

It's very important to get out of bad trades quickly. Always keep in mind that the market continually presents new opportunities. If you overstay a bad trade, chances are you'll miss the next good opportunity. Similarly, when a trade is working for you, don't inflate the potential profits. Don't expect too much from a single trade. Take your profits while they are ripe on the vine—when the momentum is still in your favor.

Everybody has good days in this business. And everybody has bad days, too. By thinking defensively all the time, you can limit the damage done on bad days. When you handle bad days well, you are on your way to becoming a good trader.

■ Pull the Trigger

Trading is not for the weak-minded. You need to do the necessary background work before the market opens, and you need to have your trading templates in place.

You need to monitor the market and anticipate 80/20 situations. And once the situation presents itself, you have to be decisive. Trading well requires a sense of urgency.

Don't fall victim to the "paralysis of analysis." You have to act when the opportunity presents itself. If you get a buy or sell signal on the template, then make the trade. Generally speaking, the better the opportunity, the shorter the time it will be available. There are many good traders in the market. When a great opportunity materializes, many of these traders will recognize the situation and act on it. As a result, the market will move quickly and decisively in one direction. If you wait too long to analyze the opportunity, it will pass you by.

■ Opinions Are for Pundits, Not Traders

Everywhere I go, people have an opinion about the stock market: on television, the Internet, and even on the golf course. It gets to the point where it's hard for me not to have an opinion. People who know I'm a trader naturally ask me about the market. I'm sure the same thing happens to many of you. Remember, whatever your opinion is, we trade 80/20 opportunities, not our opinions.

I come into each day with an open mind, ready to go long or short as the market action dictates. Based on my background work, I may think that there's more potential for the market to go in one particular direction, but I don't let that view prevent me from trading in the opposite direction if the opportunity presents itself.

■ Strictly Follow Technical Data

The financial press usually attributes every move in the stock market to something in the news, most frequently an economic report. And security analysts look at corporate fundamentals to determine whether a stock is fairly valued. I purposefully ignore both economic and corporate fundamentals. It's simply not my game.

Technical indicators and charts record all the buying and selling activity in the market, organized in a manner that allows me to spot high-probability trading situations. That's all I need to focus on to make money in the market. As a trader, you can't follow everything. Charts are very important for short-term trading because they show the underlying market psychology. And technical indicators help to time exit and entry points. Both are indispensable.

To get a better picture of market dynamics, it's valuable to assess the market one time frame greater than your trading time frame. For example, if you are trading with a 5-minute chart, use a 30-minute chart to gain additional perspective.

You want to be sure to get confirmation from technical indicators and charts before taking a position. For example, don't buy or sell a market only because prices have dropped or risen substantially and the market seems hugely under- or overvalued. Wait for the indicators and charts to signal a buy or sell.

As you gain experience with charts and technical indicators, you'll develop a sense of anticipation about changes in trend. You'll see momentum flagging, spot divergences, and sense that the balance of power between buyers/sellers is shifting from one side to the other. When you see the trend changing, get focused on your trading templates and get ready to trade.

■ Market Entry Tactics: Use Limit Orders, Buy/Sell Zones, and Position Scaling

Regardless of the time frame that you trade, it's very difficult to pick a precise top or bottom. Instead, based on your analysis, you should target a buy and sell zone where you project it's safe to be long or short.

Whenever possible, you should use limit orders to establish a position in your buy/sell zone. A limit order guarantees that you'll get in at your price or better. While it's possible that your limit order will not get filled and the market may move quickly in the direction you anticipated, I've found that rarely happens if I placed my limit order at a reasonable price.

In many cases, I'll scale into a position. For example, I may place a limit buy order for two E-minis. If I've caught the beginning of a strong move, I may purchase another two E-minis at a higher price and then perhaps another two E-minis at an even higher price.

■ Use Defensive Stops

I advocate the use of stops to limit potential losses. You can set them at specific prices or at values created by your technical indicators. You need to be disciplined about setting stops with every trade so that you don't allow a small loss to turn into a big loss.

I typically place my initial stop two points away from my entry price. Once the market moves in my favor, I move my stop to lock in a profit. I won't wait for the market to slow down or retreat before exiting. I'll get out with the momentum still in my favor. If you're trading on a longer time frame, your stops should be larger, more in the order of 5 to 10 points.

There will be times when you are right about market direction, but you're wrong on market timing. In those situations, you may very well get stopped out of your trade. There's nothing wrong with getting back in the market shortly thereafter if another 80/20 setup materializes.

If the market moves in your favor, you should adjust your stops to lock in gains. Markets can move against you quickly; you don't want to transform a nice profit into a loss. Again, if you get stopped out on a minor pullback after adjusting your stop, you can always get back in.

If a trade is showing a loss toward the end of the day, I'll liquidate the position before the market closes. I don't want to hold losing positions overnight.

I may average up or down in certain situations; however, I do not average up or down above my core position. To average down means that you buy additional stocks or contracts at a lower price after the market has dropped below your initial purchase price. To average up means you sell additional contracts at a higher price after the market has risen above your initial short position. Again, my core position is my maximum position based on my psychological comfort level. For me, it's 10 E-mini contracts.

■ Track Your Results

At the end of each trading day, I note my profits and losses (P&L) for the day, for the week, and for the month. I'm very precise in my record keeping. I feel that precision carries over into my trading and helps keep me focused. I'm always aware of how each new trade contributes or detracts from my P&Ls. By focusing on high-probability trades, my P&Ls typically show continuous growth, with a few relatively small down periods. However, the returns are not consistent.

You can extract from the market only what the market gives you, and your returns will vary depending on market conditions. You cannot demand consistency in your returns; it's just not in the nature of the business. New traders, particularly those with a background in a structured business environment, need to understand and accept that their weekly and monthly P&Ls likely will show a wide range of returns.

But while your returns will vary, you must demand consistency in your discipline and adherence to your trading rules. You should review your trades daily to determine if you acted in concert with your rules. You should reread and study your trading rules on a regular basis. Make them part of your trading DNA. They are the blueprint for your success.

■ Managing Your Trading Account

If you are showing consistent profits, for psychological reasons, it's a good idea to pay yourself something from your trading account. You deserve to be rewarded for your success. It will help to keep you motivated and give you positive feelings about your trading.

You should not intermingle your trading account with your investment account. In-and-out trading and long-term investing are two distinctly different disciplines.

By having the two activities in the same account, you may be tempted to change a trading position into an investment position, which is usually not a good idea. In addition, with the two accounts intermingled, it's more difficult to segregate the trading P&L and evaluate your trading performance.

■ Take Advantage of Market Conditions

Trending markets and trading range markets present different opportunities and require different strategies and tactics.

First and foremost, you should be aggressive in trending markets in establishing a position in the direction of the trend. Given the profit potential in a trend, you can afford to give up a tick or two to get into the market.

Be aware that prices usually move faster in downtrends than uptrends. In downtrends, protective stops get hit and investors close long positions. To avoid losses, there is often a rush to the exits. In uptrends, investors are faced with a less pressing situation: establish a new long position, add to an existing long position, or close a long position for a profit. Investors have more time to make a decision. As a result, there's a slower pace of buy orders and slower price movement on uptrends.

There are times that the market goes into what I call a "white heat" condition where prices move very rapidly, sometimes gapping up or down. If you're fortunate enough to have a position in the direction of white heat, my advice is to take advantage of the situation and close your position while the momentum is still with you. If you wait until the white heat move loses steam, it very well may gap in the opposite direction.

In trading range markets, you should be more selective in establishing a position. To the degree possible, you want to buy at the bid and sell at the offer. The profit potential in trading range markets is smaller than in trending markets, so you want to get the best possible trade location.

If a market has been in a trading range for three or four days, it's likely that the market will make a big move when it finally breaks out of the range.

In most situations, it's best to trade in the direction of the short-term trend. However, you want to avoid chasing the market. Usually, there will be a pullback where you can get a better price than jumping on a breakout.

As you gain experience in markets, you'll develop a sense of market sentiment. When the majority opinion is either bullish or bearish—and the market doesn't move in the direction of the market consensus—the market will likely move strongly in the opposite direction.

My indicators are sensitive to changing market conditions and will sometimes get me into positions a little early. Generally, that's a good thing. You get a better feel for the market once you have a position.

And assuming the indicators were right, being early usually translates into a more profitable trade.

Review the Rules Every Week

Please don't read these rules, nod your head and agree that they make sense, and then pretty much forget about them. These rules are the product of my years of experience in the markets. If I had had the rules when I first started trading, my path to consistent profitability would have been much shorter. Read the rules regularly and make them your own.

CHAPTER 4

Technical Analysis and Trading Concepts

My evolution from a struggling trader to a consistently successful trader would not have been possible without technical analysis. Technical analysis allowed me to read the market and identify trading opportunities. I examined many, many trading tools over the years and have come to rely on a dozen or so indicators.

I am a pragmatist in the selection and use of technical indicators. I want to know how they operate and respond in various market conditions. However, I'm not particularly concerned about why they operate as they do. For me, the proof is in the pudding. If they work, I'm happy. If they don't work, I get rid of them.

■ Moving Averages

Moving averages are used to emphasize the direction of a trend and smooth out price and volume fluctuations or "noise" that can confuse interpretation.

I use a 21/55/89 period moving average. These are all Fibonacci numbers. They can be used for any time frame, from a 2-minute chart to a weekly chart. I've experimented with other moving averages over the years, but have found the 21/55/89 period works best for me.

Moving averages were one of the first technical analysis tools ever developed, and they have been an integral part of my trading for years. Just because moving averages are relatively simple in their construction, do not underestimate their usefulness. When combined with other indicators, they can produce excellent trading signals.

A moving average is constructed by computing the average price of a security over a specified number of periods. For example, a 10-day moving average adds the closing price of the market for 10 consecutive days and divides that number by 10. Each day, the new closing price is added and the oldest closing price is dropped from the equation. With a new value generated each day, the moving average is displayed on a chart in conjunction with the actual market prices.

There are two types of moving averages: simple and exponential. A simple moving average weights each closing price the same. As a result, there is a lag between the simple moving average and the most recent price action. If there is a price breakout from a consolidation pattern, it will take some time for the simple moving average to catch up to the price action.

An exponential moving average (EMA) reduces the lag by placing more weight on recent prices. Charting packages calculate the EMA for you, so you really don't need to know how to calculate the average yourself. In any case, the formula for calculating an EMA is:

$$EMA = (CP \times SF) + (Previous\ EMA \times (1 - SF))$$

where   CP = Current price

              SF = Smoothing factor, which is calculated: $2/1 + N$

              N = Number of time periods selected

As you might infer from weighting multipliers, the shorter the EMA, the more weight that is placed on recent price action. A very short-term EMA, say five days, will track prices very closely. And regardless of the chosen period, an EMA will tend to track price more closely than a simple moving average.

What Moving Averages Reveal

Moving averages essentially identify the level of underlying bullishness and bearishness in the market. A rising moving average indicates the market is becoming more bullish. A falling moving average indicates the market is becoming more bearish. The sharper the slope, the greater the bullishness or bearishness.

You can also infer market sentiment from the relationship between prices and the moving average. When prices drop below the moving average, bearishness is increasing. When prices rise above the moving average, bullishness is increasing.

When you use multiple moving averages, the alignment of the moving averages is critical. Using three moving averages, a bullish alignment consists of the short-term average on top, the medium-term average in the middle, and the longest-term moving average at the bottom. A bearish alignment consists of the longest-term

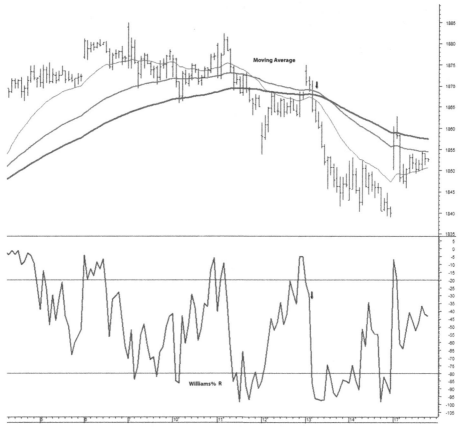

FIGURE 4.1   Moving Average: 21/55/89 Bars

moving average on top, the medium-term moving average in the middle, and the short-term moving average on the bottom.

As markets change direction, the slope of the moving averages shift and the shortest-term moving average will often cross the medium-term and long-term moving average. As short-term momentum increases, the moving averages will tend to separate. As prices settle down and volatility lessens, the moving averages will tend to converge.

Figure 4.1 shows all of these properties. On the left side of the chart, the moving averages (21/55/89) are in a bullish alignment and the prices are above all three moving average lines. Prices then fall back into the moving averages and the moving averages begin to flatten, an indication that the trend is changing. Eventually, prices drop below the moving averages, and the moving averages realign themselves into a bearish alignment. On the right side of the chart, the 21-bar moving average is sloping up, and prices have returned to the moving averages. The level of bearishness is decreasing.

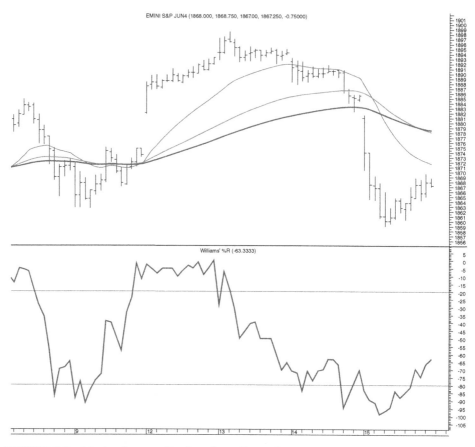

FIGURE 4.2 Moving Average: Breakout from Congestion

How to Use Moving Averages

I use moving averages in my trading, and I venture to say most other short-term traders do as well. I move in and out of the market quickly every day. By being more responsive to the most recent price movements, exponential moving averages suit my trading style.

But moving averages can also be valuable for a longer time frame. Many traders track the 50-day and 200-day moving averages to time long-term trends in the stock market and use crossover signals from the two moving averages to move in and out of stocks. In essence, when the 50-day moving average is above the 200-day moving average, the long-term trend is bullish. When the 50-day moving average is below the 200-day moving average, the long-term trend is bearish.

As I mentioned, I use the 21/55/89 period moving averages. In most market conditions, the three moving averages tend to bunch together. I am always alert for situations where the 21-day breaks out from the bunch. I will then trade in the

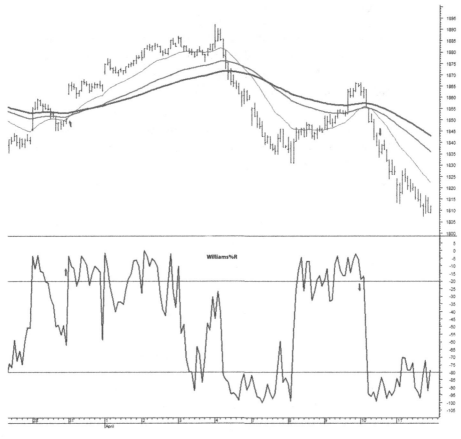

FIGURE 4.3 Moving Average: Realignment from Bearish to Bullish to Bearish

direction of the breakout. Typically, the longer the moving averages stay bunched together, the more explosive the breakout move. Figure 4.2 exemplifies this idea very well.

More commonly, I use changes in the slope lines and crossover signals. Typically, I'll look for the 21-bar moving average to begin to move more sharply up or down and to cross the 55-bar moving average and the 89-bar moving average. In Figure 4.3, a sharp change in the slope of the 21-bar line leads to crossover signals and realignment from bearish to bullish and then back to bearish.

As stated earlier, moving averages lag behind market activity. Thus, a moving average crossover signal will get you into the market only after the market has already turned. Crossovers will not identify tops and bottoms. At their best, crossovers identify change in trend direction and tradable market swings. Depending on the situation and what other signals are doing, I may trade based on the slope of the line or I may wait for the crossover signal.

MACD

The moving average convergence-divergence (commonly called MACD) is one of the most popular technical indicators. Developed by Gerald Appel in the 1970s, you can find the MACD on all standard charting packages. I've found the MACD to be very valuable in my trading.

The MACD provides both trend-following and momentum information. The primary MACD line is formed by taking two moving averages and subtracting the longer moving average from the shorter moving average. The signal line is then formed by creating an exponential moving average of the primary MACD line. On a chart, the primary MACD line fluctuates above and below a zero line and converges, crosses, and diverges from the signal line over time.

The MACD histogram is formed by subtracting the signal line from the MACD line. Like the MACD line, the histogram fluctuates around a zero line on a chart. The histogram registers a positive reading (above zero) when the MACD line is above the signal line and a negative reading (below zero) when the MACD line is below the signal line.

I use the default settings on the MACD, which are as follows: a 12-bar moving average, a 26-bar moving average, and a 9-bar moving average of the MACD line. You can experiment with settings to make them more or less sensitive, depending on your trading style. If you lengthen the settings, you'll get fewer trading signals; if you shorten the settings, you'll get more trading signals.

The MACD provides useful information about the momentum of the market. When the MACD line and the signal line are moving apart (diverging), directional momentum is increasing. When the MACD line and the signal line are moving closer (converging), directional momentum is decreasing.

■ Crossovers

Many traders use signal line crossovers as a trading signal. A signal line crossover occurs when the MACD line crosses the signal line. When the MACD line crosses the signal line on the way higher, it's bullish. When the MACD line crosses the signal line on the way lower, it's bearish. Generally, signal line crossovers work best at the beginning or middle of a price swing. In the later stages of a price swing, when prices are at an extreme and directional momentum is slowing, there may be a quick series of signal line crossovers, reflecting a battle between bullish and bearish traders.

Centerline crossovers are another popular MACD signal. A centerline crossover occurs when the MACD line crosses the zero line. When the MACD line crosses the zero line on the way higher, it's bullish; when the MACD line crosses the zero line on the way lower, it's bearish.

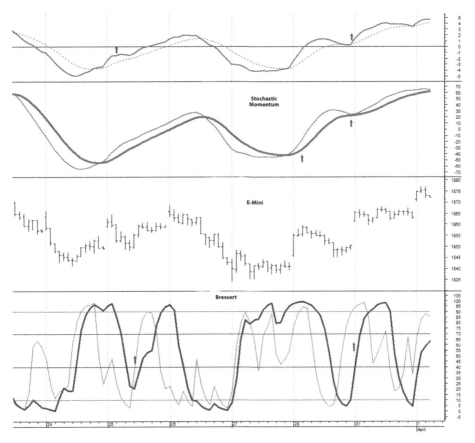

FIGURE 4.4 MACD Crossover Signals

In Figure 4.4, the uppermost chart is the MACD. As you can see, there are three occasions where the MACD line crosses the signal line. In each case, the market continued in the direction of the crossover. Notice, too, that each time the MACD line crossed the zero line, the market also continued in the crossing direction. Late in the session, the market touches the zero line—but doesn't cross it—and then continues higher.

■ Divergences

One of the most popular uses of the MACD—and indeed, any momentum indicator—is to spot divergences between price and momentum. The core idea is that when prices reach a new high or low on lesser momentum, the market is ready to move in the opposite direction.

Divergences can occur in any time frame: weekly, daily, or intraday. You can read them using the MACD line and signal line or on the MACD histogram.

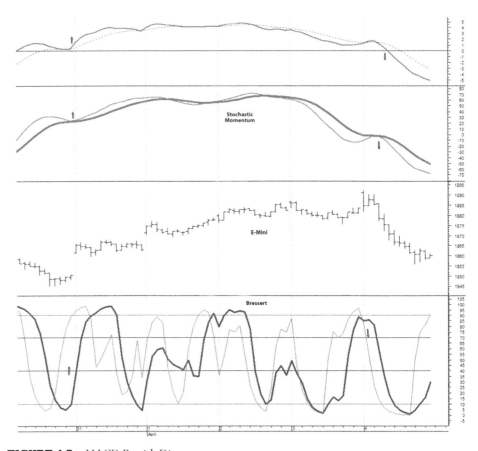

FIGURE 4.5 MACD Bearish Divergence

Some traders like to draw trend lines on the MACD lines or histogram to get a better sense of the trend in momentum.

While divergences do not always lead to an immediate price reversal, they work frequently enough that they always merit attention. When I spot a divergence, I become very interested in a possible trade and look closely at my other indicators for confirmation.

About four-fifths of the way into the session in Figure 4.5, there is a pronounced bearish divergence. The market makes a new high, but the MACD falls substantially short of its previous session high. The divergence is confirmed by similar formations in the stochastic momentum.

A word of caution about divergences in strong trending markets: When a new trend begins with a very strong initial move, it's quite possible that the next move in the direction of the trend will be more muted—and will generate a divergence signal. In those situations, pay attention to the signal line: as long as it's above the zero line in an uptrend and below the zero line in a downtrend, it's telling you that the momentum is still in favor of the underlying trend. Generally, in a strong trend, it's less risky and more rewarding to trade divergences in the direction of the trend.

◼ Williams %R

The Williams %R indicator was developed by Larry Williams. It is a momentum indicator that identifies bullish and bearish conditions and overbought and oversold areas.

The %R formula compares the current closing price of the market to the high and low of the market for a designated number of days. In essence, the indicator shows where the market is trading in relation to the upper and lower boundaries of the selected trading range.

Williams used 14 days as the setting, which is the default setting on most charting packages. If you reduce the setting, you'll speed up the indicator and generate more signals. If you increase the setting, the indicator will slow down and generate fewer signals.

The value of the %R ranges from a low of −100 to a high of 0. To register a −100 value, the most recent closing price has to be the lowest low of the designated number of days in the range. To register a 0 value, the most recent closing price has to be the highest high of the designated number of days.

Traders use the Williams %R in a variety of ways. Some use it to identify overbought and oversold conditions. They might look to buy a market when the Williams %R falls below −80, and they might look to sell a market when the indicator rises above −20. The problem with this approach is that in a strongly trending

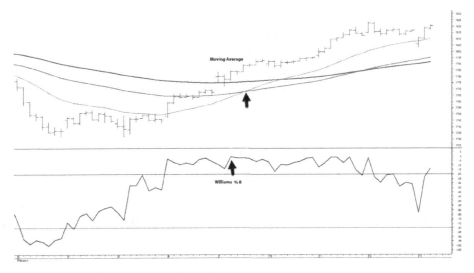

FIGURE 4.6 Williams %R, Bullish Signal

market, the Williams %R can stay at extreme levels for long periods of time. Personally, as a day trader, I have no problem going long when the indicator is overbought or going short when it is oversold—provided my other indicators are flashing buy and sell signals.

I prefer to use the Williams %R as an indicator of bullish or bearish conditions and then use other signals for confirmation to make a trade. Figure 4.6 provides a good example. A little short of halfway into the chart, the Williams %R rises above −20 and stays there for some time, which indicates the market is bullish. When the 21-bar moving average turns up and crosses the 55-bar moving average, that's the signal to go long.

▪ Stochastic Oscillator

The stochastic oscillator is another momentum indicator. It's a popular indicator used by many traders and technicians. Developed by George Lane over 50 years ago, the stochastic oscillator tracks the speed or momentum of price movements. The core idea of the indicator is that momentum changes often precede price changes.

My style of trading is to take a profitable piece from short-term price swings. I don't try to pick tops or bottoms. I don't try to predict the market. I wait for the market to confirm a directional price swing. I get in quickly. If the market stalls, I'll usually exit immediately. If the market moves my way, I'll usually take my profit prior to the completion of the price swing.

For a trade to make sense to me, the stochastic oscillator must be moving in the direction of the potential trade. Ideally, I like to see the stochastic oscillator turn up or turn down from an extreme level, with the fast line decisively crossing the slow line, and a nearly vertical ascent or descent.

The stochastic oscillator shows the location of the close in relation to the high/low range of a select number of periods. In essence, if price is closing near the top of its range for several periods, the stochastic oscillator will trend up. If the price is closing near the bottom of the range for several periods, the stochastic oscillator will trend down.

The stochastic oscillator is calculated as follows:

$$\%K = \text{Current Close} - \text{Lowest Low} \times 100$$

$$\text{Highest High} - \text{Lowest Low}$$

$$\%D = \text{Three} - \text{Period Simple Moving Average of } \%K$$

The stochastic oscillator is plotted on a 0–100 scale. The %K is the fast line and most responsive to the latest price action. The %D is the slow line. Readings below

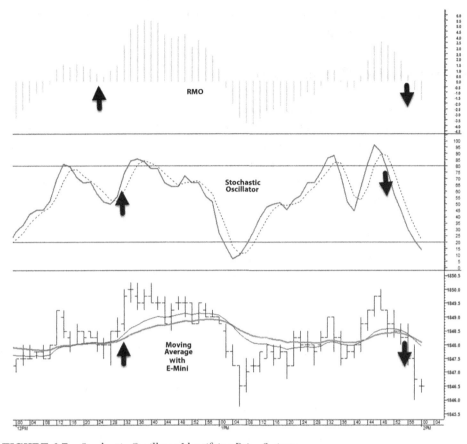

FIGURE 4.7 Stochastic Oscillator Identifying Price Swings

20 indicate the price is near its low for the time period. Readings above 80 indicate the market is near its high for the time period.

The terms *overbought* and *oversold* are used a lot in the markets, and in particular with the stochastic oscillator. Without question, markets become extended. And often, when markets reach an extreme level, some traders take profits and other traders enter new positions in expectation of a reversal, all of which can cause the market to reverse from the original trend. However, the fact that the stochastic oscillator is above 80 or below 20 does not mean a reversal is imminent. I've made a lot of money over the years being long with the stochastic oscillator above 80 and short with it below 20.

The far right side of Figure 4.7 exemplifies what I like to see in the stochastic oscillator when considering a trade. Note that it sold off from an extremely high level and moved down in nearly vertical descent, with the fast line crossing the slower line.

Also note that the bearish signal of the stochastic oscillator was confirmed by the other indicators.

■ Stochastic Momentum

Stochastic momentum derives from the stochastic oscillator. Whereas the stochastic oscillator calculates the distance between the current close and the high/low range for a chosen period, the stochastic momentum calculates the distance of the current close to the center of the high/low range for a chosen period.

Stochastic momentum originated, or was at least popularized, by William Blau in the early 1990s. Blau felt the original stochastic oscillator gave too many false signals, in part, because it was based on the high/low range. Blau felt by connecting the close to the midpoint of the high/low range, the stochastic momentum indicator would reflect market conditions more accurately and produce a higher percentage of accurate signals.

Formula

The stochastic momentum values range between −100 and +100. While I use the stochastic momentum as a means to identify the strength of the current trend, other traders use the stochastic momentum to identify when a market is overbought or oversold. Generally, when the stochastic momentum crosses +60 or −60, the market is beginning to get overextended. Readings of +80 or −80 are strongly overextended.

The stochastic momentum tends to be a little faster than the traditional stochastic oscillator. When the markets turn, it's often the first indicator in the template to flash a signal. Used alone, you would be whipsawed by too many short-term moves. But used in conjunction with other indicators in the template, it is a very powerful tool.

I use stochastic momentum primarily as a means to detect the beginning of new price swings. When it's moving sharply high or lower, and the fast line crosses the slow line, I become very interested and look to other indicators for confirmation. In addition, because it is very sensitive to recent price movements, the stochastic momentum sometimes alerts me to stay out of a trade where slower moving indicators might be flashing a buy or sell signal.

Figure 4.8 shows how the stochastic momentum works in conjunction with other indicators. Throughout the session, a change in slope and the fast line crossing the slower line coincided with tradable price swings and were confirmed by activity in the other indicators.

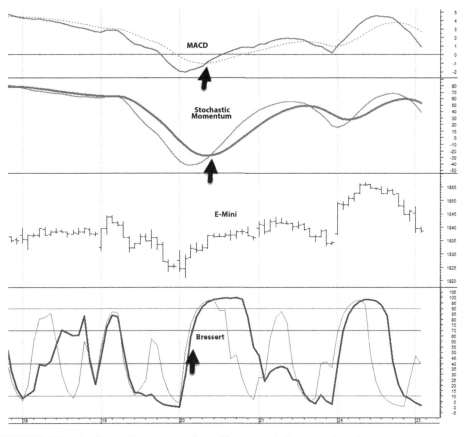

FIGURE 4.8 Stochastic Momentum: Slope Changes and Crossover Signals

■ Bressert

The Bressert is a proprietary indicator offered on the MetaStock platform. Developed by Walter Bressert, it is based on cycle analysis and shows trend direction, anticipates cycle turning points, and identifies market cycle tops and bottoms as they occur with mechanical buy and sell signals. I do not use the mechanical buy and sell signals. Instead, I use it in conjunction with other indicators. Often, the Bressert gives an early indication of a change in trend direction and possible trade. I will then look for confirmation from other indicators.

In Figure 4.9, the Bressert is the first indicator to turn (about halfway into the session) and begins to ascend on a sharp angle. The other indicators quickly confirm the move.

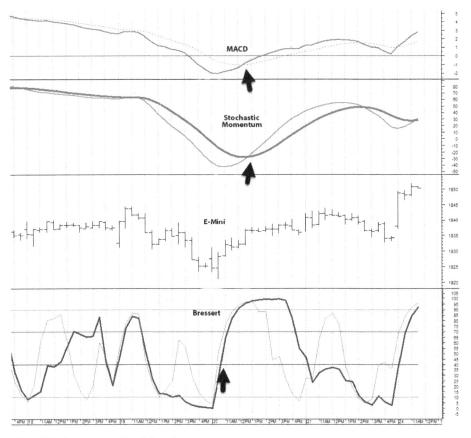

FIGURE 4.9   Bressert: Lead Signal

■ RMO

The Rahul Mohindar oscillator and its associated tools and indicators were developed by Rahul Mohindar of Viratech (viratechindia.com). Like the Bressert, the RMO is available over the MetaStock platform.

The RMO is designed to identify market direction and the primary trend. It is displayed as a histogram. A bullish signal is when the histogram moves up and crosses the oscillator's zero line going upward. A bearish signal is when the histogram moves down and crosses the zero line going down.

In Figure 4.10, the RMO starts out well above the zero line, but prices are relatively flat. About midsession, price makes a new high, but the RMO does not make a new high, indicating a bearish divergence. The divergence is confirmed on the stochastic oscillator.

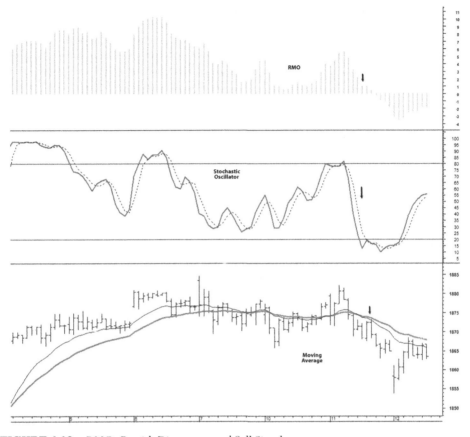

FIGURE 4.10   RMO: Bearish Divergence and Sell Signal

The RMO begins to show bearish signs and finally late in the session it crosses the zero line on the way down. This is a valid RMO signal, and it is confirmed by the other indicators.

■ Moving Ribbons

Moving ribbons combine a large number of moving averages onto the same chart. When all the averages are moving in the same direction, the trend in that direction is obviously very strong. In trading ranges, moving ribbons tend to converge on one another. As directional volatility increases, they tend to widen. When markets reverse trend, there will be a series of crossovers as the moving ribbons realign to reflect the direction of the new trend.

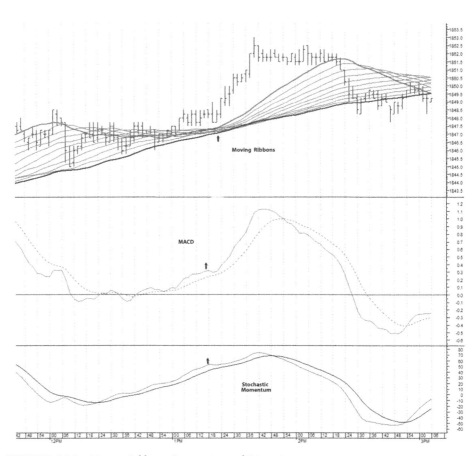

FIGURE 4.11   Moving Ribbons Converging and Diverging

In Figure 4.11, initially the moving ribbons are tilted higher in concert with the prices moving up. As prices flatten, the moving ribbons converge and there are some crossovers of the faster moving averages through slower moving averages. Then the uptrend resumes and the moving ribbons diverge and tilt higher. Toward the right side of the chart, the prices move down again. In response, some of the moving averages tilt down and cross slower moving averages. From a trading perspective, the resumption of the uptrend midway through the session was confirmed by other indicators and represented a good trading opportunity.

CHAPTER 5

Trading with the Moving Average Template

In this chapter, we'll go through a series of examples of trading with the moving average template, each starting with a chart and followed by an explanation of the trade. Let's get started.

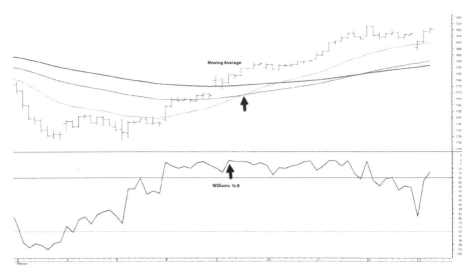

FIGURE 5.1 Moving Average Template Trade 1

I use the Williams %R a little bit differently than some of the other indicators. For a long-side trade, I want to see the Williams %R above the second line from the top. For a short-side trade, I want to see the Williams %R below the second line from the bottom.

In each case, the trade must be corroborated by a rising or falling moving average trend. Moreover, the moving averages should be aligned correctly. By that I mean, for a bullish trade I want to see the 21-period average on top, followed by the 55-period average in the middle, and the 89-period average on the bottom. For a bearish trade, I want to see the 21-period moving average on the bottom, the 55-period average in the middle, and the 89-period average on top. Very simply, this alignment shows that recent momentum, as reflected by the shorter moving averages, is moving in the direction of the potential trade. I don't follow this rule exactly in every situation. At a minimum, I want to see the two faster moving averages trending in the direction of the potential trade.

As the session opens in Figure 5.1, the moving averages are in a bearish alignment, with the fast-line, 21-period average on the bottom, the 55-period average in the middle, and the 89-period average on the top. All of the averages are sloping downward. The Williams %R is also moving down. When the %R crosses the lower line, you can put on a short-side trade.

As the session continues, the market begins to flatten and then rally. The %R follows suit. About a third of the way into the session, the %R crosses the top line and stays there, setting the stage of a potential long-side trade. When both the 21-period and 55-period moving averages turn up, I feel comfortable going long the market.

The market flattens toward the later part of the session and the %R falls below the top line. Toward the right edge of the chart, the %R again crosses the top line and the moving averages are in a bullish alignment and are trending upward. This might be an opportunity for a longer term trader, but it's too late in the day for me.

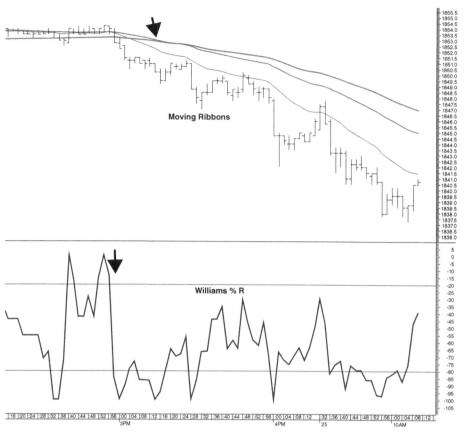

FIGURE 5.2 Moving Average Template Trade 2

The market opens flat in Figure 5.2. The %R moves into a bearish condition early on, but the moving averages do not confirm. Then, the %R spikes up, entering bullish territory, but again there's no confirmation from the moving averages.

About one third of the way into the session, prices start to decline; the %R moves sharply lower, crossing again into a bearish condition; and all three moving averages trend lower. This is an excellent 80/20 opportunity.

If you took your profits quickly on the first opportunity, there are other short-trade opportunities through the remainder of the session. The moving averages trend down and are in a bearish alignment until the end of the session. Each time the %R falls below the bottom line, you have the signal to take a short position.

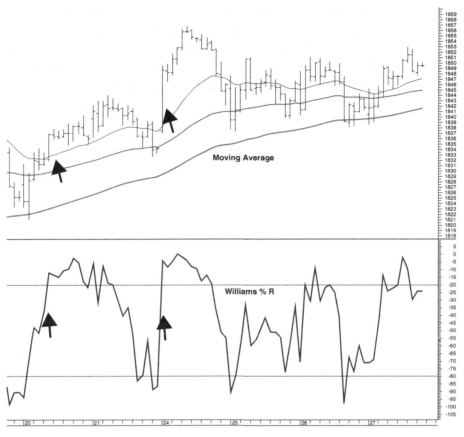

FIGURE 5.3 Moving Average Template Trade 3

Early in the session in Figure 5.3, prices start moving higher, and the %R enters bullish territory. The moving averages are in a bullish alignment, with the fastest lines above the slower lines. When the averages tilt upward, you have an 80/20 long-side trade.

The market continues higher, producing a profitable trade. Shortly thereafter, the market retreats and the %R falls below the bottom line into bearish territory. The moving averages do not confirm a short-side trade.

About one third of the way into the session, the market starts moving higher again. The %R quickly moves into a bullish condition and the fast-line moving average tilts upward again after a brief downward bend. Once that happens, you have permission to go long.

The fast-line moving average flattens out through most of the second half of the session. The %R briefly turns bearish, then bullish, and then bearish again. Just as quickly, the %R retreats from tradable conditions. In none of these cases does the moving average provide a strong enough signal to make a trade.

Finally, toward the end of the session, the %R again crosses into bullish territory. And this time, the fast line tilts upward. With the alignment of the moving averages still bullish, this is an opportunity to make a quick long-side trade. I might take this trade as there's still enough time in the session for the trade to work.

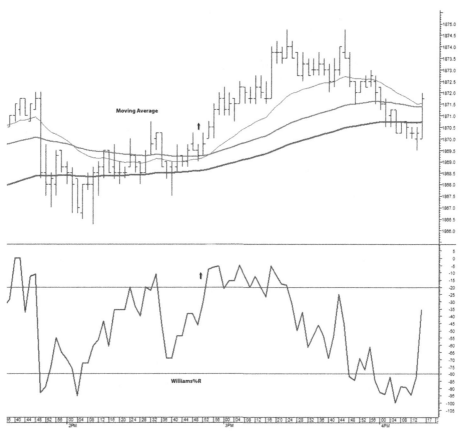

FIGURE 5.4 Moving Average Template Trade 4

The market is choppy at the beginning of the session in Figure 5.4. The Williams %R moves into bearish territory and the fast line of the moving average crosses below the medium line. However, the moving averages are not in the proper alignment for a bearish trade. What you want to see is the fast line at the bottom, the medium line above the fast line, and the slow line on the top. Without that sequence, this is not a good short trade.

Just before halfway into the session, the Williams %R moves higher and crosses into bullish territory. At about the same time, the fast line of the moving average crosses the medium line. The moving averages are in a bullish alignment and they are all tilted upward. This is an excellent 80/20 trade.

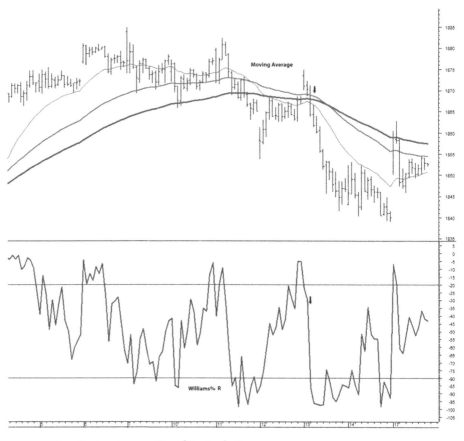

FIGURE 5.5 Moving Average Template Trade 5

The session opens with the moving averages in a bullish alignment and the Williams %R in bullish territory in Figure 5.5 but sinking fast. I would stay away from this situation and wait for more clarity.

About one fifth of the way into the session, the Williams %R rallies into bullish territory. The moving averages are still in a bullish alignment, and they are all trending upward. You could take this trade. However, at best, you would take a small profit or a scratch here. You very well might take a loss.

This is beginning to look like a market that is trying to go higher but can't get any traction. Many times, when a clear bullish or bearish trade setup has no follow-through momentum, it's a signal that the market may be ready to go the other direction.

About two thirds of the way into the session, the Williams %R begins to break sharply lower and lands in bearish territory. Prior to this, the fast-line moving average descended to the bottom of the moving average alignment and all three moving averages started to accelerate down. Particularly because of the failure of the market bulls to move prices higher earlier in the session, this is an excellent short-trade opportunity.

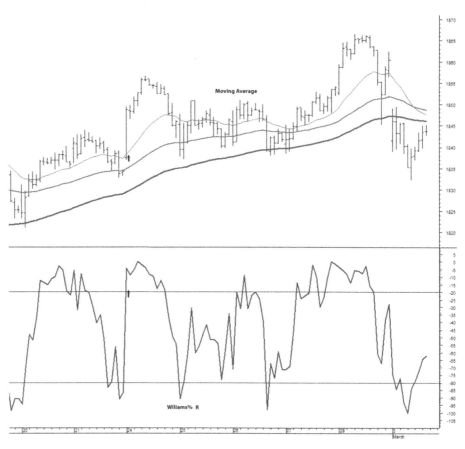

FIGURE 5.6   Moving Average Template Trade 6

This session in Figure 5.6 has a nice bullish tilt, with the moving averages in a continuous bullish alignment.

Notice the three occasions when the Williams %R moves significantly above the .20 top line. Each time, there was a profitable trade to be made. In the first instance, when the fast-line moving average begins to tilt up, it's OK to go long. The second and third instances provide stronger setups because of the sharper angle of the fast-line moving average moving higher reflects rapid upward price momentum.

This session shows there are often multiple low-risk/high-reward entry points in a trending market. If you miss the first trade or you exit quickly, you'll often have an opportunity to get back into the market.

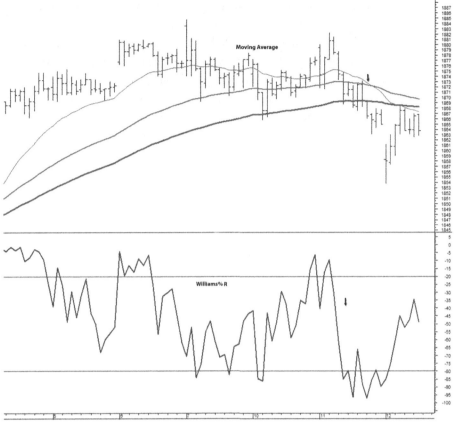

FIGURE 5.7   Moving Average Template Trade 7

Throughout most of the period in Figure 5.7, the moving averages are in a bullish alignment. The Williams %R moves into bullish territory on three occasions: at the beginning of the period, about one third in, and about two thirds in. Then, late in the session, the Williams %R moves into bearish territory, signaling the best risk/reward trade of the session.

Of course, it's always easier to read charts after the fact than in real time. Arguably, you could have gone long early in the session when the fast-line moving average began to separate from the other moving averages. With my style of trading, I would have had a scratch or a small profit on the trade.

In the second instance (about one third into the session), when the Williams %R moves into bullish territory, there's little follow-through in the price action. Given the restrained move in the moving averages, I would classify this as a 60/40 trade. Usually, my trades quickly go in the intended direction. If I were caught in a trade like this, I would get out quickly after noting the lack of price response.

In the third instance, when the Williams %R moves above the top line, the moving averages barely tilt up. Given the lack of moving average confirmation, I would stay on the sidelines. What happens next is interesting. The fast-line moving average, which has been relatively flat since midway through the session, tilts slightly down and then accelerates sharply down. The Williams %R falls dramatically and moves into bearish territory. When the faster-line moving average crosses the slower moving average, you have an 80/20 short-trade setup.

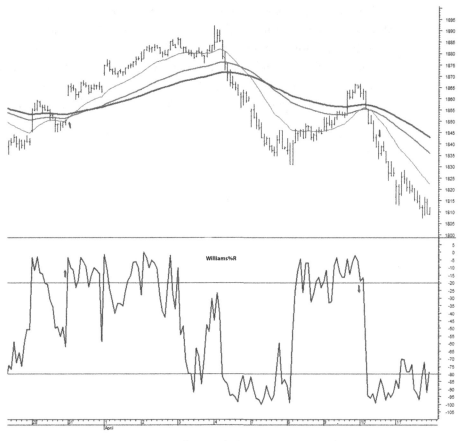

FIGURE 5.8 Moving Average Template Trade 8

Coming into this session, the moving averages are in a bearish alignment and tilting slightly downward. But the winds of change are beginning to blow. Notice the sequence of change in Figure 5.8: The Williams %R begins to move up, the market itself jumps higher, the fast-line moving average tilts sharply up, and the two slower moving averages flatten out.

After the market sells off for a few periods, it again starts moving higher. The Williams %R moves into bullish territory. The fast-line moving average crosses both slower lines, and the slower lines begin to tilt slightly upward. This is an opportune time to go long.

Around the middle of the session, the market begins a fairly steep decline. Again, the Williams %R and the fast-line moving average are the first indicators to reflect the price drop. The Williams %R remains in bearish territory. When the fast line crosses both the slower-line moving averages, you can go short.

Two thirds of the way into the session, the market begins to swing up again. The Williams %R moves into bullish territory. The fast line tilts sharply upward, and then the two slower lines tilt ever-so-slightly higher. However, after the fast line touches the slower line, it quickly retreats. Moreover, the Williams %R has now started moving down on its way to bearish territory. All the moving averages are now in a bearish alignment and moving sharply down. This is a great short-side trade.

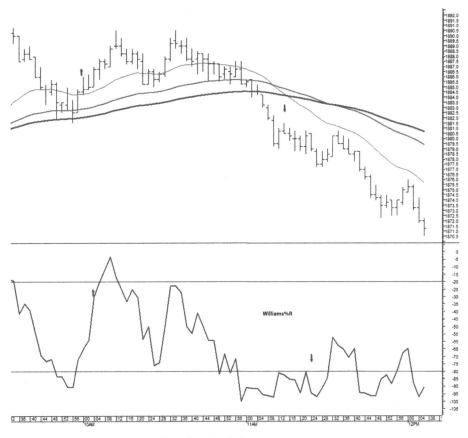

FIGURE 5.9 Moving Average Template Trade 9

In Figure 5.9, the moving averages are in a bullish alignment at the outset; however, prices are moving down and the Williams %R is also moving down and on its way to bearish territory. The market then bottoms and begins to move up. The Williams %R quickly turns bullish and the fast-line moving average flattens and begins to rise. The slower moving averages continue to tilt upward. This is a good trade to take, but you need to get in and out quickly.

Notice that through the first half of the session, the market makes two swing highs, and notice that at the second swing high, the Williams %R showed substantially less upside momentum. This is a clear and pronounced bearish divergence. This should alert you to a possible short trade.

Immediately after the bearish divergence, the market does begin to drop and the fast-line moving average begins a swing down. A little later, the downturn accelerates and the short trade emerges. The fast-line moving average crosses the two slower lines, and the slower lines turn down. The Williams %R turns bearish. This is a great trade to take.

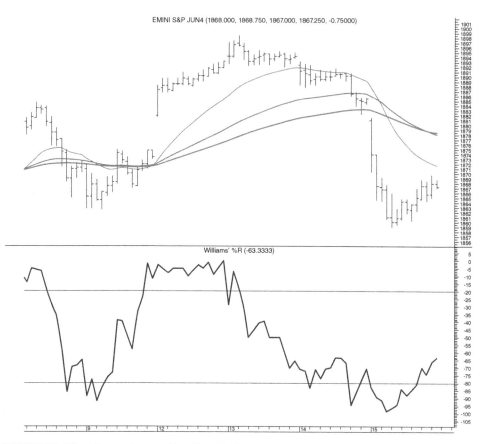

EMINI S&P JUN4 (1868.000, 1868.750, 1867.000, 1867.250, -0.75000)

Williams' %R (-63.3333)

FIGURE 5.10   Moving Average Template Trade 10

The session in Figure 5.10 begins with the moving averages in a bullish alignment, with the 21-day on top and the 55-day and 89-day underneath. But notice that the slope of the moving averages (particularly the 55-day and 89-day) is relatively flat. And with the Williams %R moving quickly from bullish to neutral territory, there's no trade to be made early in the session.

Shortly thereafter, the Williams %R moves into bearish territory, and the 21-day moving average begins to turn down. Eventually, the 21-day crosses the 55-day and 89-day. This is a bearish situation that you might be tempted to trade. However, there are two mitigating factors that make this more of a 60/40 trade than an 80/20 trade:

- The 55-day and 89-day moving averages are relatively flat, and even the 21-day is moving at a modest angle.

- The moving averages are bunched together, which indicates that the market's directional bias is fairly weak. There simply isn't a lot of energy behind this bearish move.

After the bearishness dissipates, the Williams %R moves into bullish territory about one quarter of the way into the session. Initially, the moving averages remain bunched together, until suddenly the market gaps up. The moving averages then separate and slope sharply higher. This is an 80/20 trade, but you quickly move in and out.

Toward the end of the session, the moving averages begin to slope down and the Williams %R moves into bearish territory. Prices move quickly lower. With the market moving this fast, you have to pull the trigger quickly. In this case, if you waited for the fast line (21-day) to cross both the 55-day and 89-day lines, you would have been too late. If you got in as the 21-day crossed the 55-day, you could have made a few ticks.

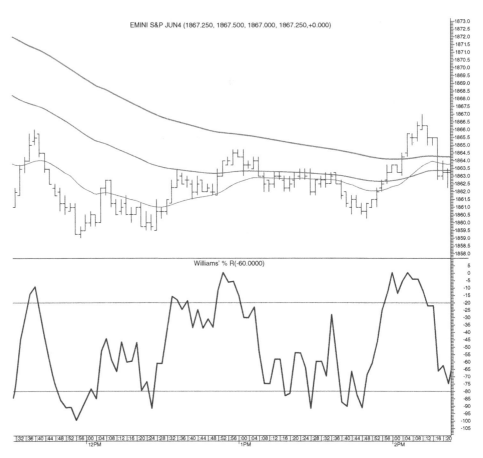

EMINI S&P JUN4 (1867.250, 1867.500, 1867.000, 1867.250,+0.000)

Williams' % R(-60.0000)

FIGURE 5.11 Moving Average Template Trade 11

As the session opens in Figure 5.11, the moving averages are in a bearish alignment, while the Williams %R and the actual prices are rising. The market then makes a swing high and starts dropping quickly.

Normally, I look for the Williams %R to move into bullish/bearish territory before putting on a trade. In this case, I would be a little quicker. The downward momentum is very strong here, as evidenced by the separation of the moving averages and the sharp downward angle in prices. As the prices fall below the 21-day moving average, I would go short.

I don't see another 80/20 setup through the remainder of this session. With the moving averages in a bearish alignment, you should focus on short trades. However, the fast-moving 21-day moving average flattens out through the last two thirds of the session, indicating a decline in volatility and, hence, trading opportunities.

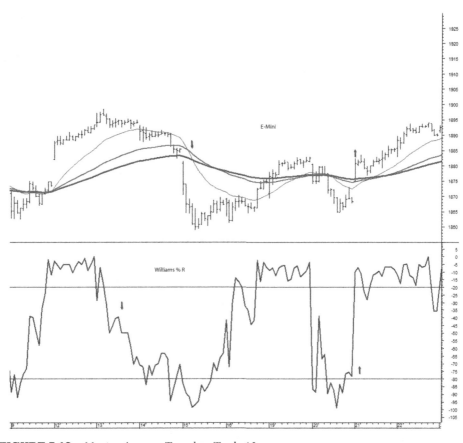

FIGURE 5.12 Moving Average Template Trade 12

Early in the session in Figure 5.12, the market gaps up. The moving averages are in a strong bullish alignment and the Williams %R is in bullish territory. This is a good trade to take even though the ensuing market move is a little tepid. If you manage the trade well, you can make a few ticks.

Just short of halfway through the session, the market breaks down. The 21-day moving average drops at a very steep angle. The Williams %R is bearish. I would go short after the 21-day moving average crosses the 55-day moving average. Given the steep downward angle on the 21-day moving average, there's no need to wait for it to cross the 89-day before putting on a trade.

Late in the session, the moving averages and the Williams %R transition from a bearish alignment to a bullish alignment. When the 21-day moving average crosses the two slower moving averages, it's safe to go long.

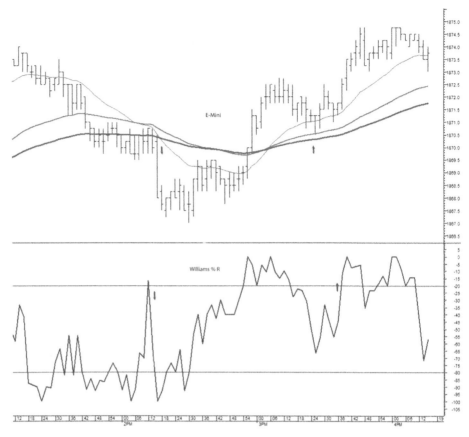

FIGURE 5.13 Moving Average Template Trade 13

At the start of the session in Figure 5.13, the moving averages are in a bullish alignment, however, the 21-day moving average is starting to turn down. After a small move up at the outset, the Williams %R begins moving down and eventually crosses into bearish territory. There is no trade to make yet, but it's clear that the market is showing a bearish bias.

Just two fifths into the session, the 21-day moving average crosses the 55-day moving average. After a quick spike up, the Williams %R starts dropping in a nearly straight line. Notice, too, the 55-day and 89-day moving averages have begun to turn down. This is a good time to go short.

About halfway through the session, the market begins to rally. The Williams %R moves into bullish territory. When the 21-day moving average crosses the other moving averages on the way up, that's a good signal to go long. However, the market begins to flatten at that point. Given the way I quickly move in and out of trades, I probably would have scratched on this trade.

Fortunately, the market provides another opportunity to go long about two thirds into the session. The moving averages have remained in a bullish alignment. When the Williams %R moves into bullish territory again, you have a signal to go long.

CHAPTER 6

Trading with the Moving Ribbons Template

In this chapter, we'll go through a series of examples of trading with the moving ribbons template, each starting with a chart and followed by an explanation of the trade.

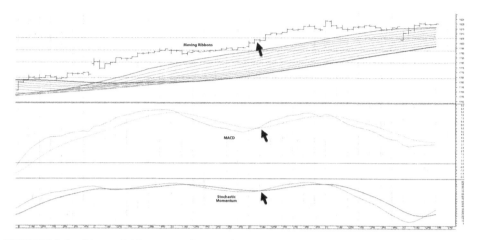

FIGURE 6.1 Moving Ribbons Template Trade 1

Early in the session in Figure 6.1, the moving average convergence-divergence (MACD) and the stochastic momentum are trending higher. However, the moving ribbons are relatively flat and converging, with the upper and lower lines moving closer together. There's no trade at this point.

About one third of the way into the session, the ribbons as a whole begin to turn up although the slow line moves slightly lower. The stochastic momentum has flattened at this point. Again, there is no trade to make.

Later, the moving ribbons expand and move higher, with all the lines participating in the move. The MACD tops out and then moves lower, and the stochastic momentum continues flat to slightly down. With the indicators in conflict, you need to sit tight.

A little past halfway into the session, the fast lines on both the MACD and stochastic momentum move higher and cross the slow lines. At the same time, the moving ribbons remain in a sold uptrend. This is the clearest trading opportunity of the session. All indicators are bullish. You should move quickly to establish a position and capitalize on the upward momentum.

As is my style, I would move my stop up as the market rises and would get out of the trade with the momentum still in my favor. If you choose to wait for one of the indicators to turn down you would get out just prior to the session high. Either way, this is a very good trade.

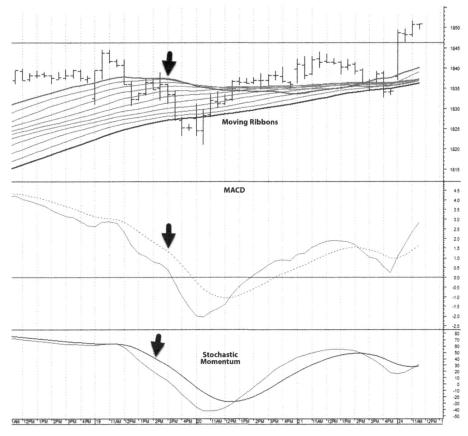

FIGURE 6.2 Moving Ribbons Template Trade 2

About one third of the way into the session in Figure 6.2, the MACD and the stochastic momentum break sharply. The moving ribbons remains flat and then eventually confirm the down move when the fast line declines slightly. At this point, you can take the trade. Given the weak response with the moving ribbons, I would classify this as a 70/30 trade.

Late in the day, the moving ribbons are flashing a bullish signal. Then, the MACD reverses course and moves sharply up. However, the stochastic momentum provides a rather weak and late confirmation. I probably would stay out of this trade.

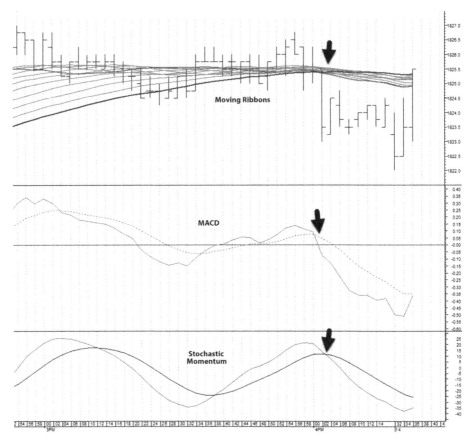

FIGURE 6.3   Moving Ribbons Template Trade 3

Through the first third of the session in Figure 6.3, the market moves sideways to slightly down. The MACD and stochastic momentum break, reflecting the bearish sentiment. However, the moving ribbons fail to confirm the bearish break. The bottom line on the ribbons trends up, while the top line is relatively flat. There simply isn't enough conviction in the market, as reflected in the three indicators, to make a trade.

A little past midsession, the MACD and the stochastic momentum bottom out and start moving higher. The price bars make three consecutive higher highs and higher lows. However, the moving ribbons remain flat. Again, there's not enough conviction for a trade.

After the price bars flatten for a period, the market again attempts to go higher. What's important here is that the MACD and stochastic momentum do not reach the highs they made earlier in the session. Thus, we have a mild bearish divergence between price and these two indicators. After the divergence, all three indicators begin to move down at very close to the same time. Here's your opportunity to make a trade. Get in quickly on the signal. Then get out quickly while the momentum is still in your favor.

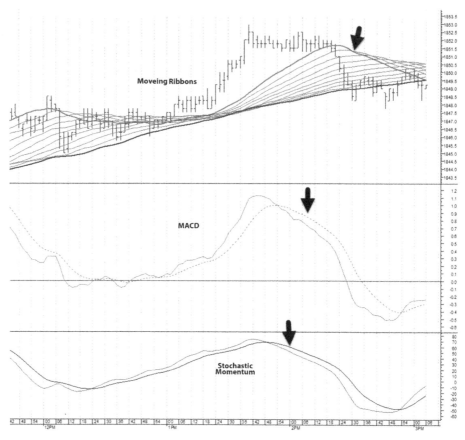

FIGURE 6.4 Moving Ribbons Template Trade 4

Early in the session in Figure 6.4, the stochastic momentum and MACD are moving lower, but the moving ribbons are converging and moving slightly higher. Later, the stochastic momentum bottoms and begins to move slowly higher. The MACD follows slowly, until about one third into the session when it moves sharply higher. At this stage, the bottom line of the moving ribbons is moving higher, but the top line remains flat. About halfway into the session, when the moving ribbons begin to expand and the top line starts trending up, you have an excellent 80/20 set up.

Later in the session, the fast lines of the MACD and stochastic momentum break lower. When the top line of the moving ribbons begins a sharp descent, there's an opportunity for a quick short trade.

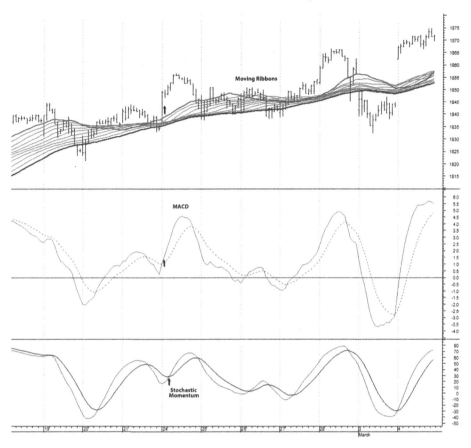

FIGURE 6.5 Moving Ribbons Template Trade 5

At the beginning of the session in Figure 6.5, the moving ribbons are moving up and the MACD and stochastic momentum are moving down. The stochastic momentum and MACD bottom and turn up, but by this time the top line on the moving ribbons has tilted down. No trade to make here.

Prices rally, fall back, and then rally again. On the last rally, the top line of the moving average ribbons turns up and the fast lines of the stochastic momentum and MACD cross the slow line. The moving ribbons are still in an uptrend, and they are now widening. This is a good trade to take.

Later in the session, there's another chance to go long when the stochastic momentum and the MACD fast lines cross the slow lines and the top line of the moving ribbons begins to move higher.

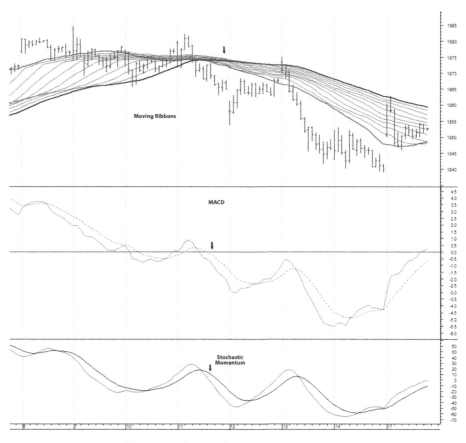

FIGURE 6.6   Moving Ribbons Template Trade 6

There are two similarly structured trades in Figure 6.6. The second works out better than the first.

For a good part of this session, the moving ribbons are rising, and the MACD and stochastic momentum are falling. Just short of the halfway point of the session, the fast lines of the MACD and stochastic momentum cross the slow lines. Then, the moving ribbons reverse course and begin to tilt down. This is a good trade to take.

The market falls quickly, enabling you to take a profit on the trade. The market then rallies, which creates another good short side set up. About two thirds into the session, the fast lines of the MACD and stochastic momentum cross the slow lines, and the moving ribbons begin to expand and tilt downward. This is another good trade to take.

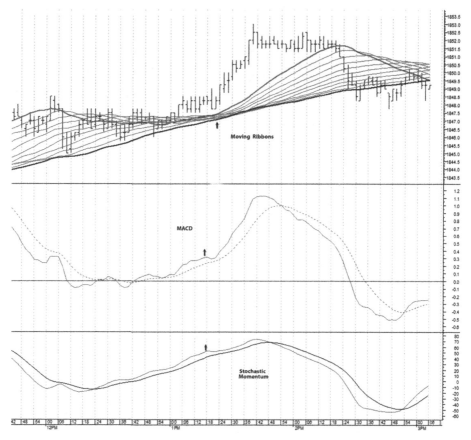

FIGURE 6.7 Moving Ribbons Template Trade 7

The market is relatively flat through the early part of the session in Figure 6.7 but slowly begins to move up. The stochastic momentum reflects the market's bullish bias first and is soon followed by the MACD. When the moving ribbons begin to tilt up, you have an 80/20 trade set up.

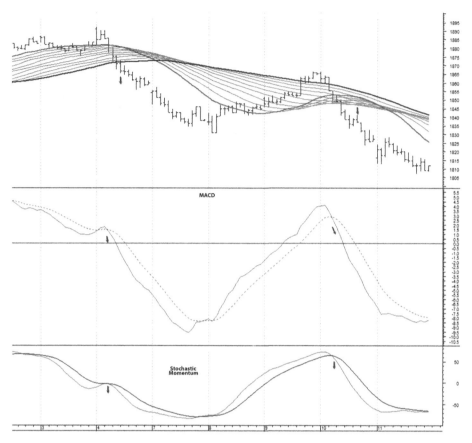

FIGURE 6.8 Moving Ribbons Template Trade 8

At the beginning of the session in Figure 6.8, the moving ribbons are trending higher, while the MACD and stochastic momentum are trending lower. About one quarter of the way into the session, the moving ribbons begin to turn down, with the fast line quickly moving through the other lines and finally crossing the bottom line. The MACD and stochastic momentum are still showing strong downside momentum. This is a good short trade to take.

Through the remainder of the session, the moving ribbons continue in a bearish pattern. The faster lines move slightly higher in concert with the stochastic momentum and MACD; however, the overall formation trends down. Toward the final third of the session, the market tops and the stochastic momentum and MACD turn down. When the fast line of the moving ribbons turns lower, you can short the market.

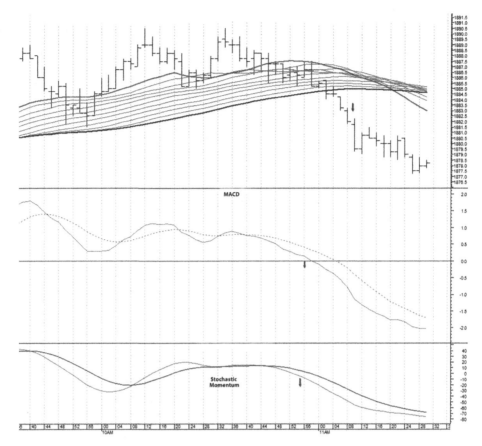

FIGURE 6.9 Moving Ribbons Template Trade 9

Toward the middle section of the session in Figure 6.9, the market makes two swing highs. The second swing high is made on lower momentum in the MACD and, to a lesser extent, the stochastic momentum. You should be looking to get short at this point.

Following the divergence, the MACD and stochastic momentum track lower, with the fast lines in both indicators crossing the slower lines. When the fast line of the moving ribbons begins to turn and cross the slower lines, and the overall formation begins to converge, you can go short.

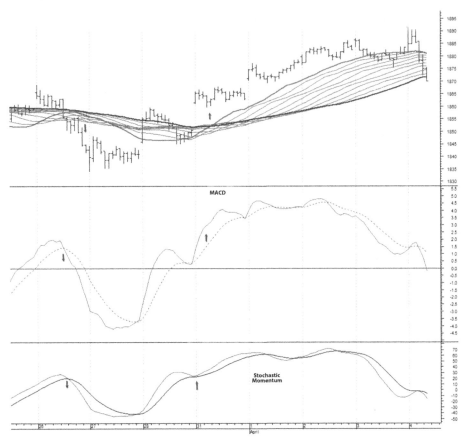

FIGURE 6.10 Moving Ribbons Template Trade 10

Early in the session in Figure 6.10, there's a brief rise in the market followed by a sharper fall. The MACD, the stochastic momentum, and moving ribbons turn bearish at about the same time. This is a good, quick trade to take.

The market bottoms and then starts rising again. The stochastic momentum and the MACD reflect the bullish move. When the moving ribbons turn positive and the fast line of the moving ribbons crosses the slow line, there is a good opportunity for a long-side trade.

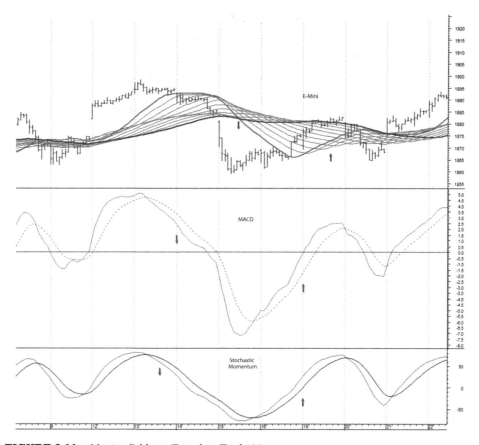

FIGURE 6.11   Moving Ribbons Template Trade 11

At the start of the session in Figure 6.11, the moving ribbons are flat and bunched together. There's no trade to make at this point.

The MACD and the stochastic momentum begin to move higher about one fifth of the way into the session. However, the moving ribbons remain flat. This is not an 80/20 trade at this point. Thereupon, the market then gaps higher and the ribbons begin to tilt upward. This is a good bullish setup.

About one third of the way into the session, the MACD and the stochastic momentum turn down. Shortly thereafter, the fast line on the moving ribbons begins to tilt slightly downward. Then the slight tilt transitions into a much sharper downward slope. This is a good bearish setup.

About two thirds of the way into the session the MACD and the stochastic momentum are moving up at a fairly sharp slope. When the fast line on the moving ribbons turns up, confirming the other two indicators, there is another bullish setup.

Finally, about four fifths of the way into the session, the market makes a swing low on weak momentum, as demonstrated by the MACD. While this is not a classic divergence pattern because the swing low did not exceed the previous swing low, the fact that the downside momentum was so weak indicates that sellers are losing conviction. I would look for a bullish situation to emerge.

Sure enough, the market gaps higher. The MACD and stochastic momentum turn up and the moving ribbons tilt slightly higher. When the fast-line moving average turns higher, it's a good situation to go long.

CHAPTER 7

Trading with the Bressert Template

In this chapter, we'll show a series of examples of trading with the Bressert template, each starting with a chart and followed by an explanation of the trade.

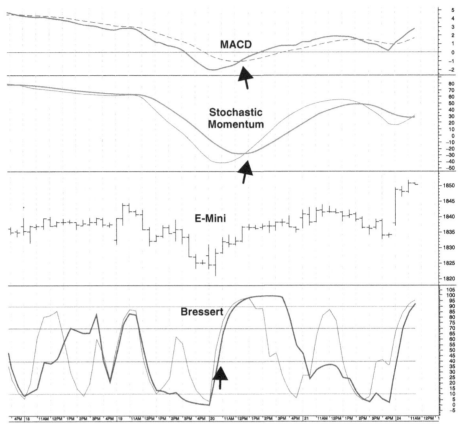

FIGURE 7.1 Bressert Template Trade 1

The session opens in Figure 7.1 with the MACD and stochastic momentum flat to slightly down and the Bressert moving lower. The Bressert quickly reverses and moves higher, but there's no change in the other indicators.

About one third of the way into the session, the Bressert has peaked for a second time and begun to fall. At the same time, there's a breakdown in the stochastic momentum and MACD. The only shortcoming to this setup is that there isn't a decisive bearish crossover of the fast lines through the slow lines in the stochastic momentum and MACD. Still, this is a valid short-trade setup.

About midway through the trading session, the selling momentum has eased and the market again turns and goes higher. The Bressert is the first indicator to turn and is quickly followed by the MACD and stochastic momentum. This is a solid 80/20 trade from the long side.

On the right side of the chart, at the very end of the session, all three indicators move sharply higher at about the same time. I wouldn't take this trade because I almost never carry positions overnight. It's a risk I'm unwilling to take. However, if you are trading on a longer time frame, you may want to take some end-of-day setups. If you are interested in holding positions overnight, you should establish off-hours trading stops.

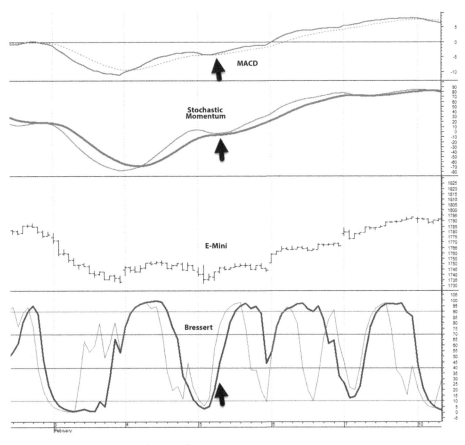

FIGURE 7.2 Bressert Template Trade 2

Early in the session in Figure 7.2, there was a good trade to the downside. After peaking initially, the Bressert broke early, leading the way. The MACD and stochastic momentum quickly confirm the move, giving you the justification to place a short position. The market moves down quickly. I would get out of the trade while the momentum is still in my favor.

About one third into the session, the MACD and the stochastic momentum start moving up and continue moving up for the duration of the chart. However, the Bressert indicator is moving down during the early part of the session at the same time the MACD and the stochastic momentum are moving up. Eventually, the Bressert bottoms out and begins to rise. This is the time to take the trade.

This is a slow-moving trade, with the market moving sideways initially. The market does not break down, however, so you could hold this trade with a close stop and get a good portion of the up move.

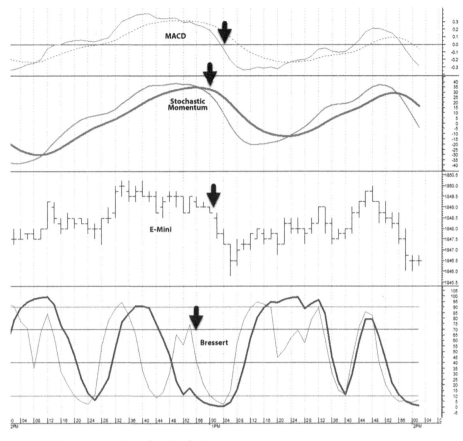

FIGURE 7.3 Bressert Template Trade 3

Midway through the session in Figure 7.3, the MACD and the Bressert start down at about the same time. The stochastic momentum indicator quickly follows, producing a good trade setup. The key is to strike quickly once the trade is confirmed. The market trends lower for three consecutive bars, giving you the opportunity for an immediate profit on the trade.

Late in the day, there's a short trade as the market begins to drop. The Bressert moves first, with both the fast and slow lines breaking simultaneously. The MACD and the stochastic momentum indicators quickly confirm the move. If you strike quickly here, there's a nice potential profit. However, even if you're a bit late, it still is a good trade.

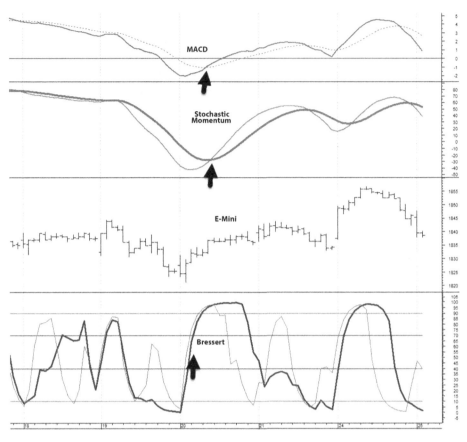

FIGURE 7.4 Bressert Template Trade 4

Through the first two fifths of the session in Figure 7.4, the MACD and stochastic momentum trend lower. The Bressert is somewhat volatile. As long as the MACD and stochastic momentum are in a bearish mode, you want to look for confirmation from the Bressert to put on a trade. Specifically, you want to see both Bressert lines moving in the same direction to confirm the trade.

There are two instances early in the session where all three signals are moving down. In the first instance, about one fifth of the way into the session, the MACD and stochastic momentum are declining at a weak angle and the Bressert is moving down. Note that you don't have a decisive bearish crossover move with the MACD and stochastic momentum at this point. This is more of a 60/40 or 55/45 trade. I wouldn't take it. If you do take the trade, you need to be in and out quickly. The Bressert then reverses, rallies, and starts falling again. At this time, the MACD and stochastic momentum break sharply down. This is a solid trade that enables you to profit from the swing high and the ensuing move down.

Shortly thereafter, both lines of the Bressert bottom and move sharply higher. Then the fast lines of the stochastic momentum and MACD turn higher and cross the slow lines. This is a high-probability long-side trade.

About four fifths of the way into the session, there's another bullish setup, similar to the previous trade. The MACD turns higher and is quickly followed by the Bressert and stochastic momentum.

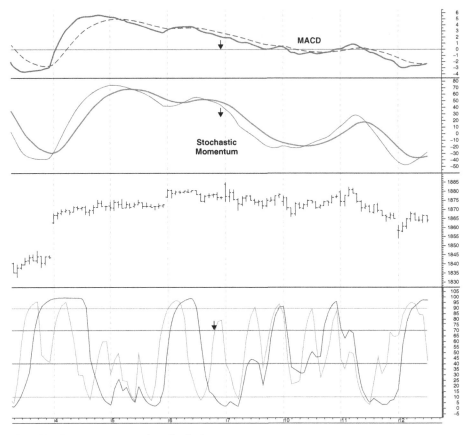

FIGURE 7.5   Bressert Template Trade 5

This is not an easy period to trade.

The market spikes higher as the session opens in Figure 7.5. The move happens so fast that there isn't any time to even think about trade using my methods.

The market then flattens and about one third of the way into the session, the MACD and stochastic momentum slowly trend down. The fast lines of the MACD and stochastic momentum cross over, creating a bearish situation. By this time, however, the Bressert has bottomed and flattened out. I don't see a good trade here.

Interestingly, each time the market tries to go up through the remainder of the session, the momentum as reflected in the MACD and stochastic momentum is progressively weaker.

About halfway into the session, the fast lines on both the MACD and Stochastic Momentum cross the slow lines and both indicators begin to accelerate to the downside. Based on our criteria, this is a good trade to take. However, the market stays flat to slightly down for quite some time. If you held on to the short position, you would eventually be rewarded. If you liquidated the initial short position for a small profit or scratch, you could get back in about four fifths of the way into the session when all the indicators break at the same time.

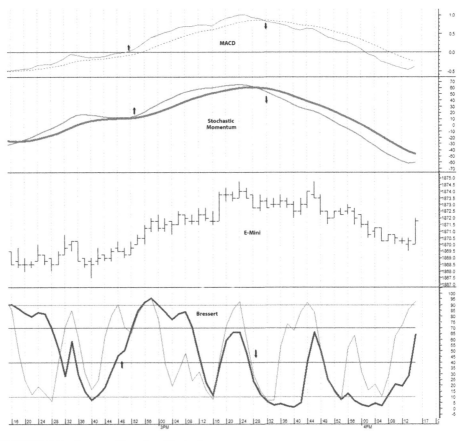

FIGURE 7.6   Bressert Template Trade 6

The session opens with the market fairly flat in Figure 7.6; however, the MACD and stochastic momentum are trending upward, while the Bresert is cycling down. Clearly, there is no trade to take here.

About one third of the way into the session, the Bressert turns up. And the stochastic momentum, after going flat, renews its bullish trend. This is a good 80/20 set up.

About three fifths of the way into the session, the Bressert begins to decline and the MACD and stochastic momentum quickly follow. This is a reasonable trade to take, although the market spikes up slightly before it begins to decline.

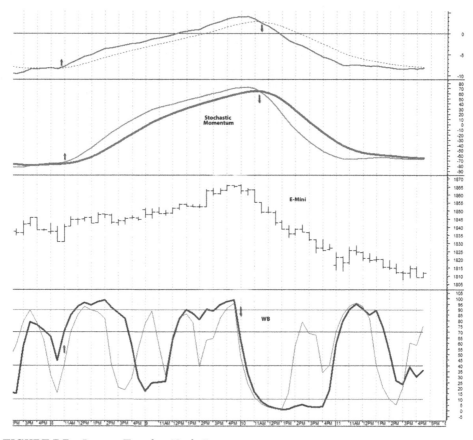

FIGURE 7.7 Bressert Template Trade 7

Early in the session in Figure 7.7, the MACD line crosses the signal line, the stochastic momentum fast line crosses the slow line, and the Bressert indicator turns sharply up. With all three indicators showing decisive bullish movement, there is an 80/20 trading setup.

Midway into the session, the market peaks and starts to descend. All three indicators flash sell signals: the MACD line crosses below the signal line, the fast line of the stochastic momentum crosses below the slow line, and the Bressert indicator drops very sharply. This is a great 80/20 short-side trade.

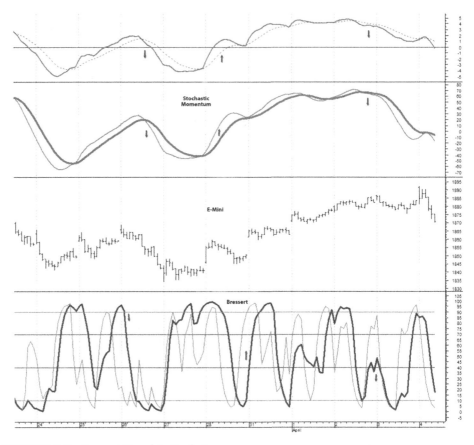

FIGURE 7.8 Bressert Template Trade 8

About one third of the way into the session in Figure 7.8, there's a nice downward break in all three indicators. Notice that the Bressert is the first indicator to turn and is quickly followed by crossovers in the MACD and stochastic momentum indicators. This is a good trade to take.

A little past halfway into the session, there are bullish crossovers in both the MACD and stochastic momentum. Shortly thereafter, the Bressert begins to cycle higher. This trade gets you in at the beginning of a long price swing.

Late in the session, the MACD and the stochastic momentum begin to decline and experience bearish crossovers. Following a weak upside cycle, the Bressert begins to cycle down. The trade works for a few bars before the market reverses. You need to be nimble and exit quickly.

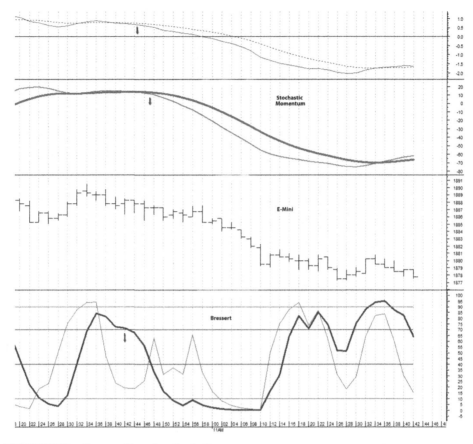

FIGURE 7.9 Bressert Template Trade 9

After an early up move in Figure 7.9, the market moves in a flat to slightly down pattern. The Bressert cycles down, and after a few more bars, the MACD and the stochastic momentum begin to move lower as well and generate downside crossovers. As you can see, this trade works out very well.

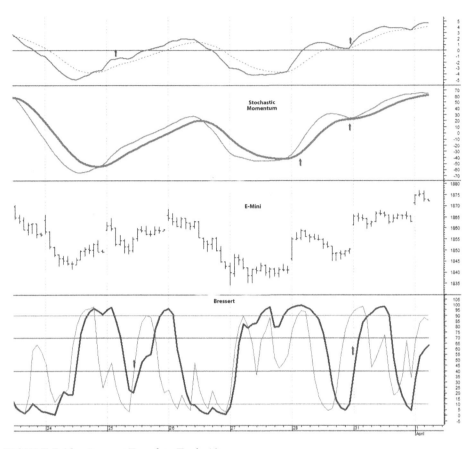

FIGURE 7.10   Bressert Template Trade 10

About one fifth of the way into the session in Figure 7.10, there are bullish crossovers in the MACD and the stochastic momentum. However, the Bressert by now has flattened near the high point of its range. There's no trade here.

After that, the Bressert quickly cycles down and begins rising again. So, at this point, all three indicators are signaling that the market is going higher. This is a good trade to take.

About four fifths of the way into the session, both the MACD and stochastic momentum touch their reference lines and accelerate higher. The Bressert is also cycling higher. So, again, you have a good long-side trade.

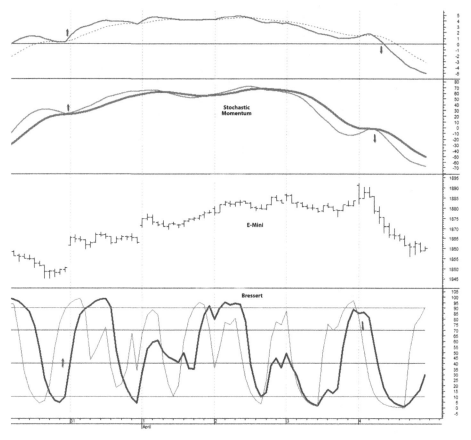

FIGURE 7.11 Bressert Template Trade 11

Toward the later stage of the session in Figure 7.11 is a very good trade setup. Notice first the bearish divergence when the market makes a new session high, but none of the indicators follow suit. The MACD, stochastic momentum, and the Bressert all make lower highs. This is a powerful sign that upside momentum is exhausted and the market is ready to decline.

Shortly thereafter, all three indicators turn sharply lower. This is a very clear 80/20 setup. You should have no hesitation taking this trade.

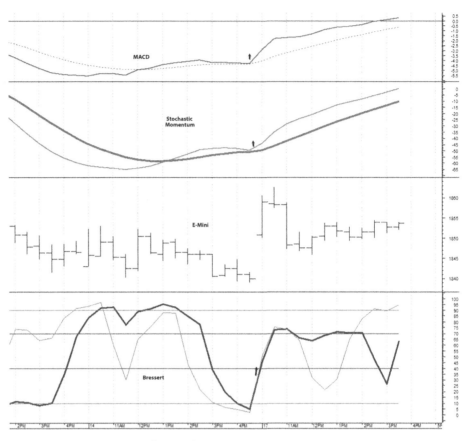

FIGURE 7.12   Bressert Template Trade 12

The session opens with the MACD and stochastic momentum displaying a bearish tone in Figure 7.12. But the Bressert—after cycling down—is flat, so there isn't a high-probability trade here.

The market then remains in a fairly tight range. The Bressert cycles up and then flattens. The MACD and stochastic momentum are also relatively flat.

Finally, the market gaps up on the opening of a new trading day a little past halfway on the chart. The Bressert cycles upward and the stochastic momentum and MACD both turn sharply higher. While I normally don't trade this close to the opening, I consider this an 80/20 trade given the strength in all three indicators.

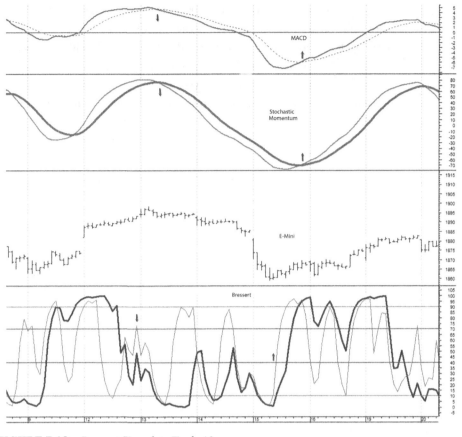

FIGURE 7.13   Bressert Template Trade 13

A multiday session covering seven days of trading is seen in Figure 7.13. At the outset, the Bressert is rallying, while the MACD and the stochastic momentum are declining. Nothing to trade at this juncture.

On the 12th, about one fifth of the way into the chart, the market gaps up and all three indicators flash bullish signals. I would take this trade. The market slowly grinds higher the rest of the day, and you could get out at any time before the close with a small profit.

On the 13th, about one third of the way into the session, the MACD, the stochastic momentum, and the Bressert all turn down. Again, I would take this trade. Note that the market goes flat the rest of the day. You might have scratched on this trade or made a small profit or loss. While the trade didn't work out, I would take this type of setup time and time again.

About halfway into the session, on the 14th, the market is in a tight trading range for the third consecutive day. However, the MACD and stochastic momentum continue to show weakness. The Bressert also is weak early in the day, and with all three indicators pointing down, a short trade is justified. Unfortunately, if you're looking for a quick profit like I do, this trade would also be a scratch. If you have a slightly longer-term perspective, you would be rewarded as the market breaks at the end of the day. Indeed, if you're flat going into the last couple of hours of trading, there is a great short opportunity as all three indicators again flash substantial weakness.

The next good trade occurs around midday on the 16th, about three fourths of the way into the chart. The MACD, the stochastic momentum, and Bressert accelerate higher. The bullish condition and rising prices persist into the next day.

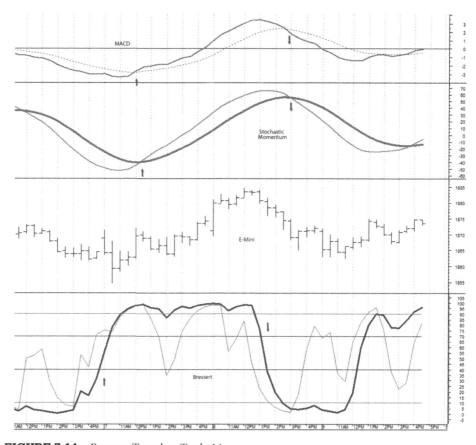

FIGURE 7.14   Bressert Template Trade 14

There are two 80/20 trades displayed on the chart in Figure 7.14.

About one-fourth of the way into the chart, both lines on the Bressert begin to move up. At that point, the MACD and stochastic momentum are in the process of bottoming out. When the fast lines on both of these indicators cross the slower lines (note the Bressert is still bullish), you can go long. The trade works out very well.

A little past halfway into the session, the Bressert begins to move sharply down. A little while later, the fast lines on the MACD and the stochastic momentum cross the slower lines, creating a clear short-trade setup.

CHAPTER 8

Trading with the RMO Template

In this chapter, we'll go through a series of examples of trading with the Rahul Mohindar oscillator (RMO) template, each starting with a chart and followed by an explanation of the trade.

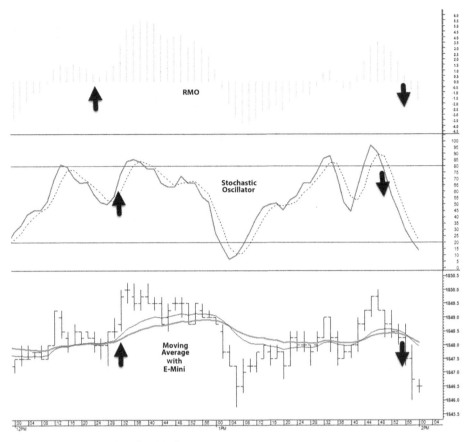

FIGURE 8.1 RMO Template Trade 1

The session in Figure 8.1 opens with the moving average relatively flat and the stochastic oscillator and RMO moving higher. The market is in a trading range, and there's little momentum behind the initial attempt of the market to go higher.

About one fourth of the way into the session, the moving average, stochastic oscillator, and RMO all accelerate higher. This is a clear 80/20 situation and a good trade to take.

After the swing high in the first one third of the session is reached, the market falls back. The stochastic oscillator and RMO reflect the fall back, but by the time the moving average confirms the move, the other indicators are in an oversold area. I would not take this trade.

The RMO and stochastic oscillator bottom about halfway through the session and begin rising, but the moving average remains flat and does not confirm the move.

Toward the end of the session, the RMO forms a bearish divergence, when the late-day session price high is made on weaker RMO momentum than the previous price high. The stochastic oscillator breaks sharply. When the moving average turns down, you have confirmation from all three indicators and a solid 80/20 short-trade opportunity.

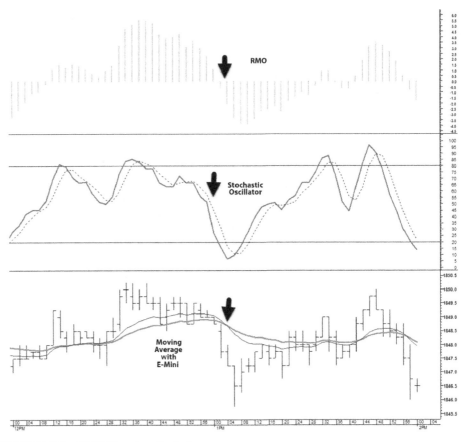

FIGURE 8.2 RMO Template Trade 2

About one-third of the way into the session in Figure 8.2, all three indicators begin to move up at about the same time. You need to catch the trade quickly, as the market moves sharply higher and then flattens. If you don't catch it early, let it go.

After the market makes a swing high, the stochastic oscillator and the RMO begin to turn. The gradual decline in these indicators then accelerates and is confirmed by a downturn in the fast moving-average line. This is a nice short-trade opportunity. Again, you have to move fast.

Late in the session, the stochastic oscillator and moving average begin to rise at about the same time, and the RMO eventually confirms. The market moves progressively higher for the next several price bars. Then, just as quickly, the market turns down again, and the decline is reflected in all three indicators.

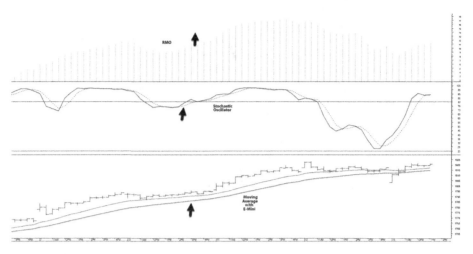

FIGURE 8.3 RMO Template Trade 3

At the beginning of the session in Figure 8.3, the moving average is moving up, and the RMO is above the 0 line. These are bullish conditions, and we only need to wait for the stochastic oscillator to confirm. Early on, however, the stochastic oscillator turns down. We have to be patient, monitor conditions for change and continuity, and wait for a good opportunity. Finally, when the stochastic oscillator turns up, that's a good opportunity to go long.

As the session progresses, the stochastic oscillator flattens and then turns down. At the same time, however, the RMO remains far above the 0 line, and the moving average is still trending higher. Conditions continue to be bullish, and you want to look for an opportunity to buy the market.

When the stochastic oscillator turns up (a little before the halfway point of the session), you can put on a trade. At that point, everything is in place. The moving average, the stochastic oscillator, and the RMO are all trending higher. This is an 80/20 trade.

The market's upward momentum begins to dissipate toward the later part of the session. The moving average flattens, and the stochastic momentum breaks sharply down. There's not sufficient unanimity among the indicators to consider going short. And when the stochastic momentum reverses late and trends higher, the flattened moving average prohibits taking a late, bullish trade.

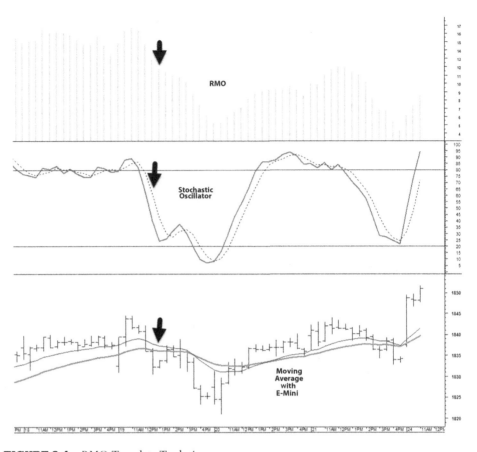

FIGURE 8.4 RMO Template Trade 4

The session in Figure 8.4 opens with the RMO and stochastic oscillator at high levels but moving in a relatively flat angle, paralleling the flat price movement in the actual market. It looks like a market ready to break, but we need to wait for confirmation from our indicators.

One third of the way into the session, the RMO and the stochastic oscillator break sharply, and the fast line of the moving average tilts down. This is a strong 80/20 short setup, particularly because the market is dropping from overbought conditions, as reflected in the RMO and stochastic oscillator.

Just past the halfway point of the session, the stochastic oscillator and RMO are moving higher again. When the fast line of the moving average tilts up and then crosses the slow line, you have a bullish trade setup. However, given that the stochastic oscillator is approaching overbought levels, this is more of a 60/40 trade.

About two thirds of the way into the session, the RMO and the stochastic oscillator form bearish divergences as the swing price high is made on weaker

RMO and stochastic momentum than the previous price high. Both the RMO and stochastic oscillator then break lower. The fast line of the moving average does begin to tilt down; however, it's a weak move, and it is not confirmed by the slower line. I wouldn't take this trade.

At the end of the session, there's a quick move up in all three indicators. Again, I wouldn't take the trade, but it might be an opportunity for a longer-term trader.

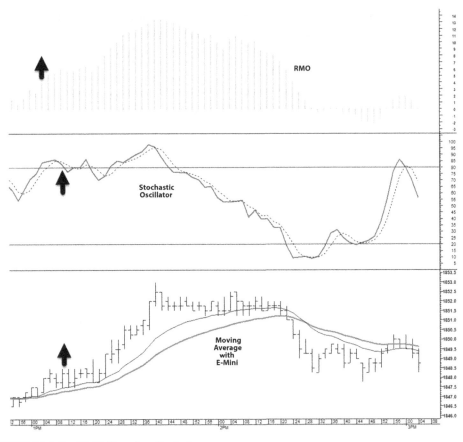

FIGURE 8.5 RMO Template Trade 5

Early in the session in Figure 8.5, the stochastic oscillator moves sharply higher, followed quickly by the RMO. When the moving average begins to tilt upward, you have confirmation and a good 80/20 trade.

After moving strongly higher, the market flattens. The stochastic oscillator and RMO begin to move down. The moving average continues rising. There's no trade in this situation.

When the moving average turns down about two thirds into the session, you can take this trade. However, by this time, the stochastic oscillator is approaching oversold conditions, so proceed with caution. Use a tight stop.

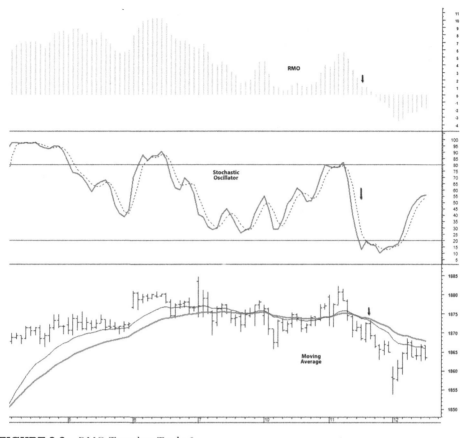

FIGURE 8.6 RMO Template Trade 6

There are no solid trade setups until late in the session in Figure 8.6. Early on, the stochastic oscillator and moving average are in conflict. About one third of the way in, the stochastic oscillator and RMO begin to decline, but the move is not confirmed by the moving averages.

An important thing to see here is the divergence that develops about three quarters of the way into the session. The price rallies; however, the RMO and the stochastic oscillator fail to reach to the levels they achieved on the previous session high. This is a bearish signal.

After the divergence, the stochastic oscillator and RMO drop dramatically and the fast-line moving average crosses the slow line. This is a solid 80/20 trade.

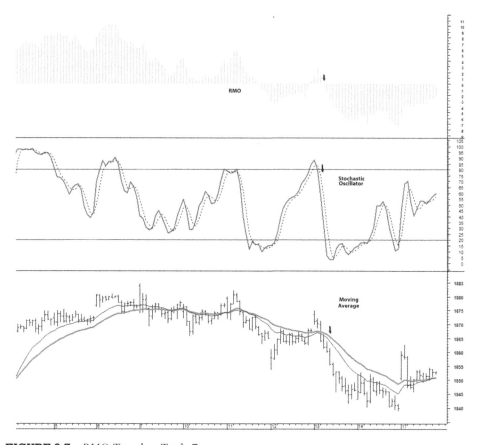

FIGURE 8.7 RMO Template Trade 7

The session in Figure 8.7 opens with the moving averages going higher, the stochastic oscillator going lower, and the RMO flat. Nothing to do here.

About midway through the period, the market tries to go higher but gets little traction and then starts down. The RMO and stochastic oscillator catch the move first, and the moving average soon follows.

About four fifths of the way into the chart is the best trade of the session. The RMO, stochastic oscillator, and moving average break down simultaneously. The fast line of the moving average accelerates, creating separation from the slow line. This is an 80/20 trade.

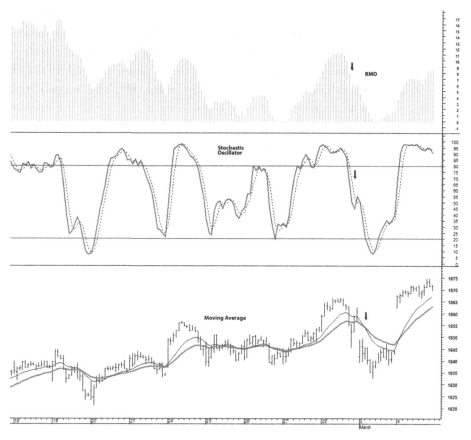

FIGURE 8.8 RMO Template Trade 8

There are several trades available on the chart in Figure 8.8, which represents two weeks of market activity. In each instance, all three indicators move in the same direction. And in each instance, the trades are profitable, provided you follow my approach of getting in and out of the market quickly.

About one fifth of the way into the session, the RMO and the stochastic oscillator break down sharply. The moving average tilts down gently in contrast to the sharper moves of the other two indicators. And the fast line of the moving average doesn't cross the slow line until the move is well under way. I would classify this as a 70/30 or 60/40 trade.

The market then bottoms and heads upward. The RMO and stochastic oscillator turn bullish. However, the moving average again is slow to respond. And by the time the fast-line moving average crosses the slow line, the stochastic oscillator is in overbought territory. I would stay away from this trade.

About two fifths into the session is a much better trade setup. The moving average, stochastic oscillator, and the RMO all rise at the same time. While the move happened at the market opening of the 24th and quite likely was a response to an economic report or other news, the response from all three indicators was very strong, indicating that follow-through was likely. This is a good trade to take.

About four fifths into the chart is the best trade of the session. The stochastic oscillator leads the way, turning up, and is quickly followed by the RMO and the moving average. This is a solid 80/20 trade.

Finally, at the very end of the session is a good short-side trade. The stochastic oscillator and RMO turn very bearish. The moving average tilts down, as well. A good time to short the market is when the fast-line moving average crosses the slow-line moving average.

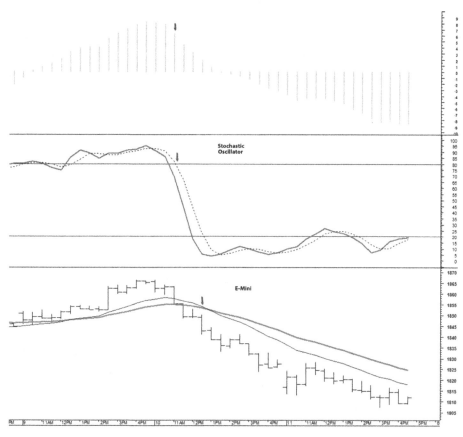

FIGURE 8.9 RMO Template Trade 9

The market opens in Figure 8.9 with the stochastic oscillator and moving averages in a relatively flat movement and the RMO slowly moving higher. The market price, stochastic oscillator, and moving average then start moving higher also, but with the stochastic oscillator at such an extreme level, this is not a good opportunity to go long.

A little bit later, the RMO and stochastic oscillator begin to turn down and are quickly joined by the moving averages. When the fast-line moving average crosses the slow line, you have a good short-side trade setup.

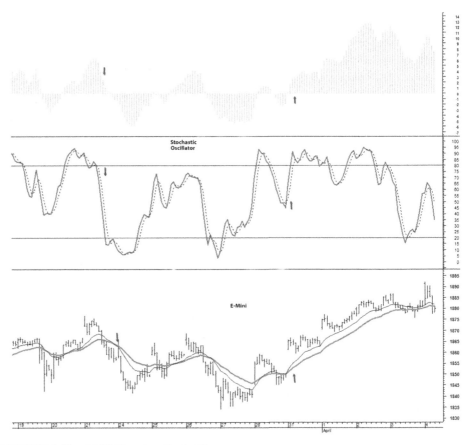

FIGURE 8.10   RMO Template Trade 10

At the beginning of the session in Figure 8.10, the moving averages are in a bullish pattern, the stochastic oscillator is descending, and the RMO is stagnant above the zero. Not much clarity here.

The market then sells off a bit and then rallies to a session high. At that point, the stochastic oscillator quickly begins to drop from an overbought level and the RMO begins to trend down. When the fast-line moving average crosses the slow-line moving average, a short-side trade emerges.

Just short of halfway into the chart, there's another bearish trade setup. The stochastic Oscillator and RMO drop sharply and are soon followed by the fast-line moving average crossing below the slow line.

A little past halfway into the chart, the market makes a swing low on very weak momentum, as reflected in both the RMO and the stochastic oscillator. While this is not a classic divergence signal because price did not make a new low, it does indicate that the downside momentum is quite weak at this point.

Following the weak swing low, the three indicators move upward at about the same time. This is a very strong trade, and the market responds with an extended rally.

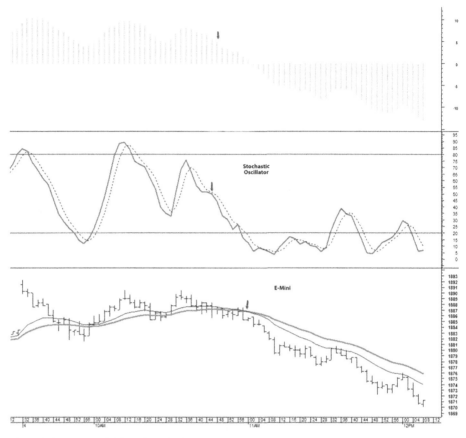

FIGURE 8.11   RMO Template Trade 11

The market is in a trading range through the first half of the session in Figure 8.11. Notice, however, that throughout the first half, the moving average is in a bullish alignment. On two occasions during this period, the RMO and stochastic oscillator turn higher and produce quick in-and-out trading opportunities. I wouldn't classify these trades as 80/20 opportunities, however, because the bullish tilt on the moving averages is very slight.

About halfway into the chart, the best trade on the session appears following a bearish divergence where price reaches the previous session high, but the RMO and the stochastic oscillator fall well short of their previous highs. Both the stochastic oscillator and RMO then break sharply. When the fast-line moving average crosses the slow line, you have clearance to short the market.

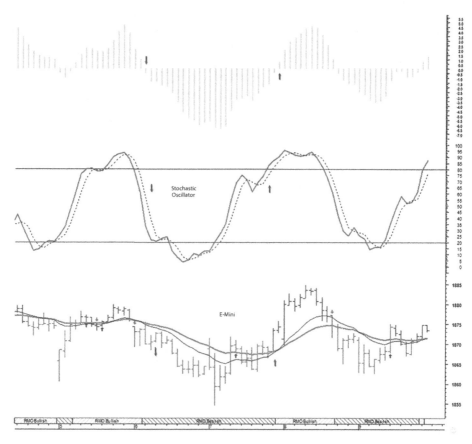

FIGURE 8.12 RMO Template Trade 12

Early in the session in Figure 8.12, the moving average is moving in a flat to slightly weaker manner. The RMO is also looking weak. However, after a slight turn down, the stochastic oscillator is moving higher. There's no trade to take here, but it's clear the market has a bearish flavor.

About one fourth of the way into the session, the RMO and stochastic oscillator form tops and then begin moving quickly lower. When the moving averages confirm the move, it's a good situation to go short.

The market forms a bottom about halfway through the session and then turns up. The RMO and stochastic oscillator start climbing. When the fast-line moving average crosses the slow line, there's a good bullish trade setup.

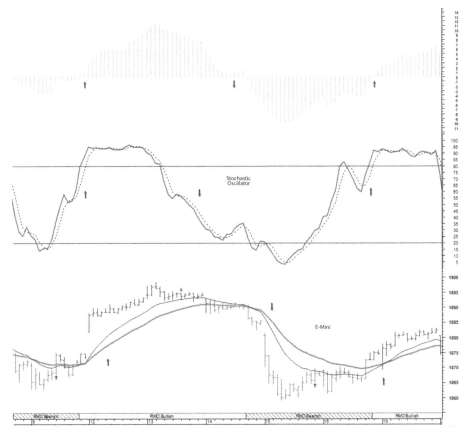

FIGURE 8.13   RMO Template Trade 13

At the start of the session in Figure 8.13, the market is clearly bearish. The RMO and stochastic oscillator are trending down. When the fast-line moving average crosses the slower line, everything is lined up to go short. The trade likely would result in a small profit or scratch.

The market gaps up about one fifth of the way into the chart, and all the indicators turn bullish. Notice the separation between the fast- and slow-line moving averages, a clear indication of strong upside momentum. This is a good trade to take.

About two thirds of the way into the chart, the market starts falling rapidly, and all three indicators turn very bearish. I would go short when the moving averages begin separating and the fast-line moving average begins to descend at a very sharp angle.

Toward the end of the chart, a bullish situation develops. You first see the upward momentum building on the RMO and stochastic oscillator. When the fast-line moving average starts turning up, you can go long.

CHAPTER 9

A Day of Trading

No one can accurately predict the market. There are simply too many variables. A seemingly perfect trade can go asunder as a result of a natural disaster, an unexpected political development, or a host of other factors. You need to acknowledge and respect the risk that is always present in the market.

My templates measure market activity and help identify high-probability trading situations. Notice I said *help* identify high-probability trading situations. My approach is not mechanical; there's always an element of interpretation involved.

It's much harder to read charts in real time than at the end of the day. In real time, you have many 60/40 situations where the market is showing a bullish or bearish bias, but you don't have all the signals lined up to make a trade. At various times during the day, you may feel impatient, fearful, or greedy. It's a challenge to remain objectively immersed in the market without feeling some level of emotional discomfort. You have to constantly discipline yourself to act on the basis of your objective analysis and not on the basis of your feelings.

It helps me to think that while I can't predict the market with absolute certainty, I can manage the market in real time. By managing the market, I mean the following:

- I objectively gather information through the prism of my templates.

- I anticipate what needs to happen to create an 80/20 trade.

- When the 80/20 situation unfolds, I put on a trade with no hesitation and with a close stop-loss.

- I take my profit or loss quickly, without emotion, and get ready for the next trade.

Remember, most of the time the market lacks clarity. Bulls and bears are in a constant battle for market control. Long-term, medium-term, and short-term traders are looking for opportunities in their particular time frames. One trader's short-term selling opportunity may be a long-term buying opportunity for another trader.

I read the market with my indicators. Throughout the day, I ask myself:

- Are the indicators flat, trending, or somewhere in between?

- Are the moving averages separating or converging?

- Are any divergences between price and momentum developing?

- Are the indicators confirming each other, or are they in conflict?

- What is the next most likely 80/20 trading opportunity?

By keeping a running dialogue in my head, I'm able to stay on top of the market in real time and anticipate new opportunities. The nature of the market is that great opportunities occur time and time again, but they disappear very quickly as nimble traders jump in and drive prices substantially higher or lower. You want to be on the forefront of those trades, and the only way that's possible is by staying actively in touch with the market throughout the day.

To provide a better idea of the internal dialogue and my trading decision process, I'll focus here on two of days of trading: May 14 and 15, 2014.

By way of background, the stock market was in the mature phase of a long-term bull market that began in March 2009. Several times during that period, the market showed signs of weakness, leading many traders and prognosticators to warn that the end of the bull market was imminent. Each time, the market rallied to record highs. As we approached May 14, the market was slowly churning higher but with very little conviction and very little volatility—not exactly the ideal situation for short-term trading.

I went into May 14 with an open mind, but with a slight bearish bias. Several indicators flashed bearish signals on the 13th: the RMO, stochastic oscillator, stochastic momentum, moving average convergence-divergence (MACD), and Williams %R (see Figures 9.1, 9.2, 9.3, and 9.4). I envisioned three scenarios: (1) the market breaks early and a strong selling day ensues; (2) the market breaks early, but the move fails and a strong buying day ensues, or (3) the market remains locked in a trading range for most of the day but breaks or rallies after lunch. As a trader, you need to be alert to all possible scenarios.

At the opening of the 14th, the market was flat, extended down a bit, and then rebounded a little. The shorter-term moving averages were relatively flat; the longer-term moving averages were tilted slightly higher, reflecting the long-term bearish trend. Many of the other indicators continued to look bearish. But despite the bearish tone, the market was not ready to break.

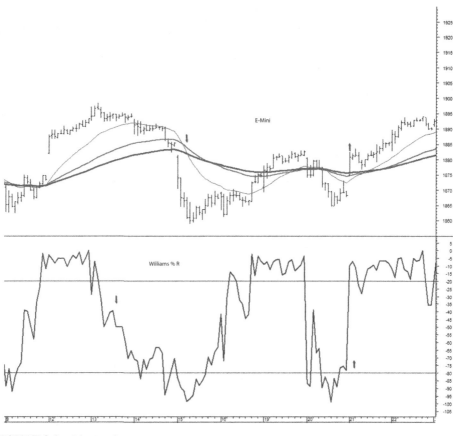

FIGURE 9.1 Moving Averages

As the morning progressed, the market established a progressively narrower trading range. In recent days, volatility had been diminishing, and there were few trading opportunities. Usually, the stock market provides one or two good trading opportunities every day. That wasn't the case lately, and I was getting a little frustrated.

Markets can stay in trading ranges for a long period of time and you can lose a lot of money trading false breakouts. At the same time, when markets decisively break out of a range, they often move substantially in one direction. Despite my frustration, all my experiences told me to sit tight, monitor the market closely, and be ready for the next trade.

Toward the end of the day, around 2:30 P.M., the market finally broke. Here's what I saw:

- The 21-period moving average turned down, and the 55-period and 89-period quickly followed.

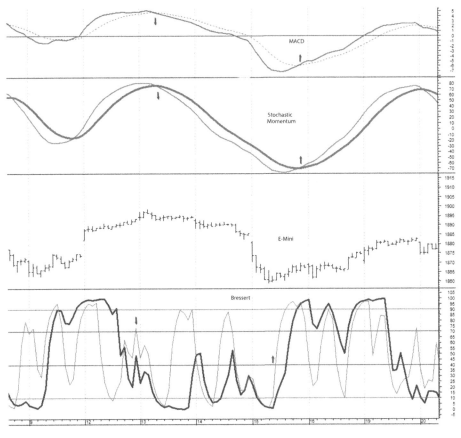

FIGURE 9.2   Bressert

- The Williams %R went negative.

- The RMO went negative.

- The stochastic oscillator went negative.

Accordingly, I went short at 1886.30. I took my profit just before the close at 1883.00.

After the breakdown on the 14th, I expected a weak market and new short-trading opportunities on the 15th. Of course, anything can happen overnight to change the dynamics of the market. A positive earnings announcement from a market leader or a bullish economic report could change the tone of the market and generate a rebound on the 15th. But assuming no significant news developments, I was alert for a weak opening and early morning selling.

Normally, I don't trade the opening. I usually wait for the market to establish an opening range and then monitor my indicators for trading setups. In this situation, however, I was prepared to go short very early on the 15th.

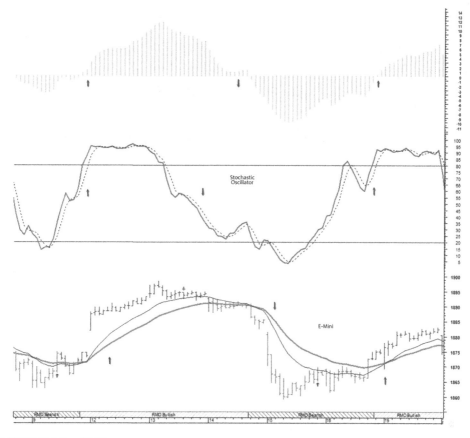

FIGURE 9.3 RMO

Notice that at the close on the 14th, every indicator on all four templates was strongly negative. This alone is reason to go short on the opening if the market opens lower than the close on the 15th. Moreover, in concert with the set-up, I'm thinking about the mind-set of portfolio managers, investors, and traders. After witnessing the breakdown of the market on the 14th, who would jump in and start buying stocks on the morning of the 15th? Clearly, the downside momentum had not abated. Even investors who believed the long-term bull market was still in force would most likely wait for the short-term selling to ease before buying more stocks. And those who feared the bull market was dying most likely would be sellers on the 15th.

The market opened on the 15th at the lower end of the previous day's range, and almost immediately the market began selling off. With all my indicators pointing down, coupled with the weak opening, I shorted the market at 1878.50 at around 9:40 A.M. In keeping with my practice of grabbing quick profits, I closed the position at 1868.25.

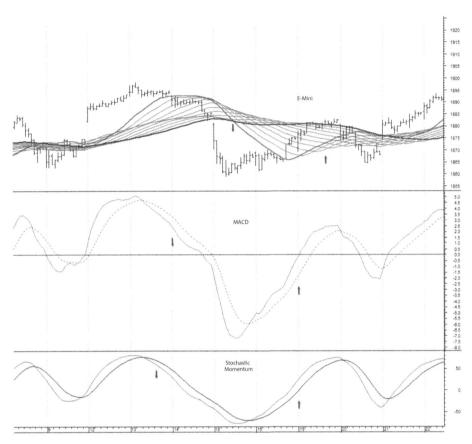

FIGURE 9.4 Moving Ribbons

The market continued lower that day and actually continued lower for the next three days. Do I regret taking my profit quickly and leaving a lot of money on the table? Not at all. I would do exactly the same trade again if given the chance. I use tight defensive stops and expect trades to move quickly in my direction. Then, once the trade goes my way, I'll get out of the market. I've done this time and time again, and I've been able to make a good living at this for many, many years.

About MetaStock Pro Templates

Dick Diamond's preferred charting platform is MetaStock Pro (intraday version). MetaStock Pro is a robust and powerful charting utility, ideal for charting, scanning, and plotting the custom indicators used in Dick Diamond's trading strategies. As such, it is important that you know how to apply and use these setups within the software. Specifically, there are four customized Dick Diamond "templates" that must be imported or created in MetaStock Pro:

- Template 1 (Walter Bressert)

- Template 2 (moving ribbons)

- Template 3 (RMO)

- Template 4 (moving averages)

A "template" contains all the information in a chart or layout excluding the base security. When a template is applied to a security (either to an existing open chart or when loading a chart), all of the pertinent indicators and custom views will apply, too, based on the template's information. Each template is saved as a file with a .wmt extension.

If the information from a template came from a single chart, then a chart is created when the template is applied. If the information came from a layout, then a multichart layout is created. You can also create a default template that is always used when a new chart is created.

Creating the Dick Diamond Templates

A template is created from the information in a chart or a layout. Once that chart or layout appears as you'd like, use the "Save As" command in the File menu to save the template. If you create a template when a multichart layout is selected, a multichart template is created. If you create a template when a single chart is selected, a single-chart template is created.

Here are the steps to follow when creating a new template:

1. Open MetaStock.

2. In the Power Console, type in a symbol (e.g., ESc1), then click Next.

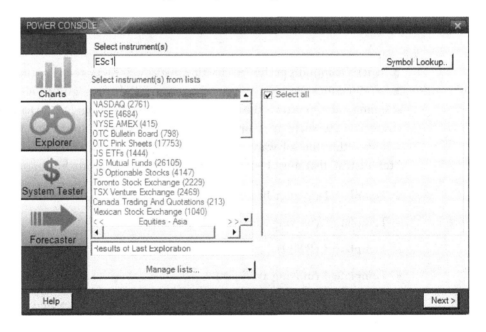

3. On the next page of the Power Console, you can choose a range of options. For the purpose of setting up a new template, you can utilize the default settings by simply selecting Open Chart.

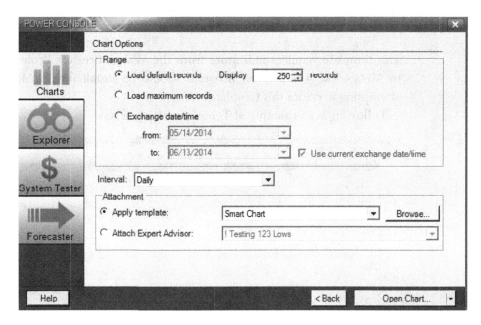

4. After the basic chart is open, you can add the indicators and settings for your template. Make the desired changes to the chart by adding the indicators and specifications included in the template. (A full listing of the constituent parts of each of the five templates will follow).

5. When the template is complete, choose Save As from the File menu.

6. Choose Template from the Save As drop-down list.

7. Type the name of the template in the File Name box.

8. Click the Save button.

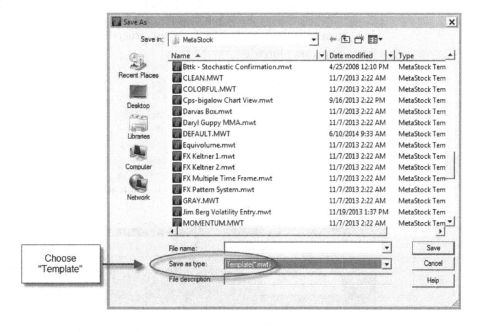

■ Template 1: Walter Bressert

This template requires indicators from the Walter Bressert Profit Trader add-on to MetaStock. This add-on program should be installed into MetaStock before attempting to create this template.

Following is an example of Template 1 for reference:

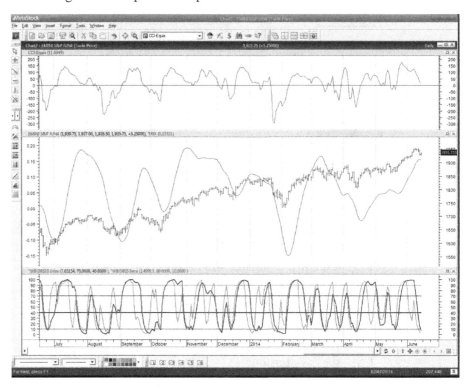

First, open a blank chart. Notice from the preceding reference example that there are four indicators plotted:

1. CCI-Equis (14 periods)

2. TRIX (12 periods, close)

3. "WB:DBS10 Intra (default settings)

4. "WB:DBS5 Intra (default settings)

To plot these indicators on the chart, first locate the indicators from the drop-down menu on the top tool bar:

Template 2: Moving Ribbons

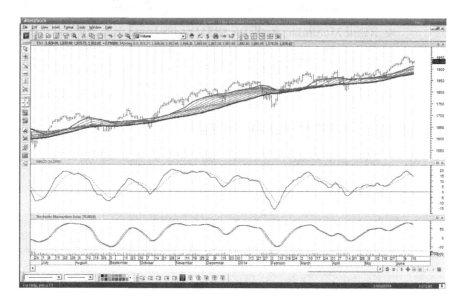

First, open a blank chart. Notice from the preceding reference example that there are three indicators plotted:

1. Moving ribbons (time periods set to 20, spacing 5, ribbons 12)

2. MACD (standard 12,26,9)

3. Stochastic Momentum Index (14,9,9), moving average 3

Template 3: RMO

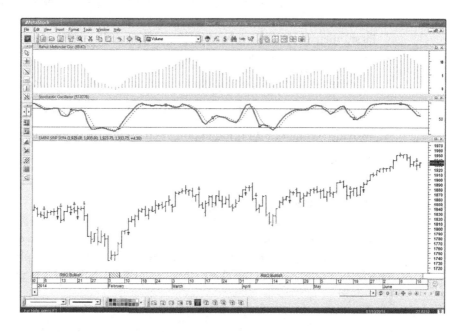

First, open a blank chart. Notice from the preceding reference example that there are two indicators and then buy and sell indicators:

- Rahul Mohindar oscillator (RMO) displayed in histogram format
- Stochastic oscillator (14,3,3)
- Chart with the RMO Expert Advisor attached

■ Template 4: Moving Averages

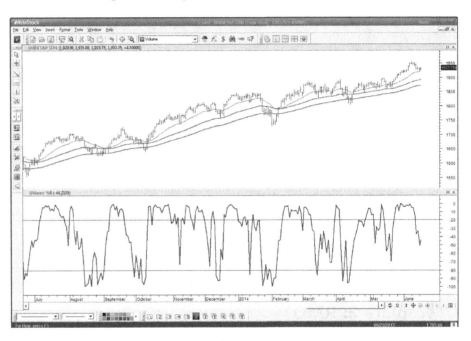

First, open a blank chart. Notice from the preceding reference example that there are four indicators plotted on the chart:

1. Moving average: 21-period exponential moving average, close
2. Moving average: 55-period exponential moving average, close
3. Moving Average: 89-period exponential moving average, close
4. Williams %R, 14

■ Applying an Existing Template

Templates can be applied to a chart on the screen when you open a smart chart from the Open dialog, or when you create a new chart. When a template is applied to a chart, the template uses the chart's base security for all charts in the template.

If the template was created from a single chart, then a chart is created when it is applied. The name in the affected chart's title bar will appear as "Chart 1" with the security name following.

To apply a template to an open chart:

1. Right-click on the chart.

2. Choose Apply Template from the shortcut menu.

3. Choose the desired template from the Apply Template dialog.

To apply a template when loading a security:

1. Open the Power Console.

2. Enter the security you want to open.

3. On the Chart Options page, it will ask if you want an attachment. Select the template under Apply Template.

4. Choose Open Chart, and it will open the chart for you.

■ Making Changes to a Template

Changes are made to a template by opening (applying) the desired template, making the changes, and resaving the template to the same file name.

To make changes to an existing template:

1. Apply the template you want to change to a security or chart.

2. Make the desired changes.

3. Choose Save As from the File menu.

4. Double-click the name of the template file you are editing.

5. Click Yes when asked if you want to replace the existing file.

■ Saving a Template

Templates are saved using the Save As command in the File menu. If you want the changes you have made to a template to be retained, you must save the template using the Save As command. You can also save a template as the default template. The default template is automatically applied to all newly created charts.

To save a template:

1. Choose Save As from the File menu.

2. Choose Template from the Save As drop-down list.

3. If you are editing a template and want to save the changes to the same template name, double-click the name of the template file.

4. If you are saving a new template, type a name in the File Name box and click Save.

■ The Default Template

You can control how a newly created chart appears using the "default template." The default template is a special template that is exactly like a regular template except that MetaStock automatically applies it to newly created charts. The default template that is shipped with MetaStock is just a single chart with high-low-close price bars and volume.

The default template is named DEFAULT.MWT, and it is stored with your other templates at c:\MyDocuments\MetaStock. This means that the default template can be applied at any time just like a regular template. For example, you could change the default template so that candlesticks and a moving average are always plotted when a new chart is created.

To quickly make the information in the currently selected chart the default template, right-click the chart and choose Save as Default Template.

Click here to save the chart information as the default template

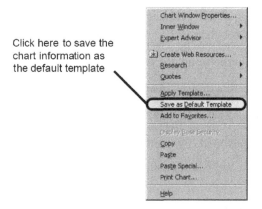

To edit the default template:

1. Choose New from the File menu, and select Chart.

2. Double-click any security to chart listed in the dialog.

3. Make the desired changes to the chart.

4. Right-click on the chart and choose Save as Default Template from the shortcut menu.

■ Creating the Diamond Work Space

Dick Diamond will view the charts in a 2 and 30 format. Once you have set up the above templates, you can easily create the two-view format and look at the 2- and 30-minute together:

1. Open any chart with the template to be used. For the purpose of this example, we will use the moving average template.

2. With the chart open, use the Window, New Window Function in MetaStock. This will allow the program to duplicate the existing chart.

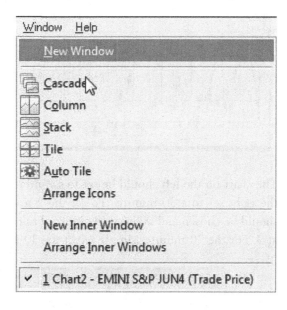

3. There will be two of the same chart open. To view the two charts side by side, choose the Column button.

4. Now that the charts are displayed side by side, the time frames can be changed to the 2- and 30-minute time frames. Select the Periodicity button on each chart.

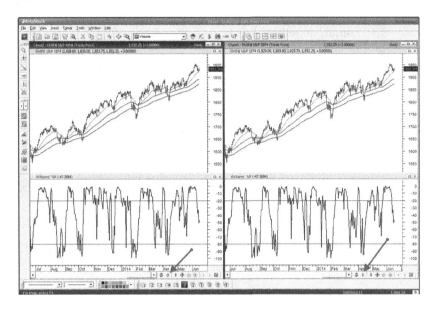

5. The chart on the left should be set to a 2-minute time frame, and the chart on the right set to a 30-minute. To set the 2-minute chart, the Custom interval should be chosen and then set the interval as minute. The multiplier should be at 2. For the 30-minute, simply select the 30-minute from the drop-down.

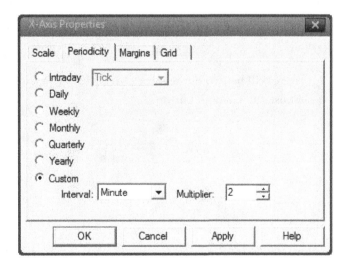

6. Verify that your time frames are correct. MetaStock Pro will show you the time frame in the top right-hand corner of your chart.

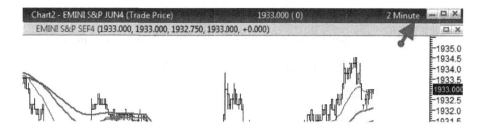

7. You will need to save this as a layout with the two charts open side by side. To do this, go to File | New | Layout.

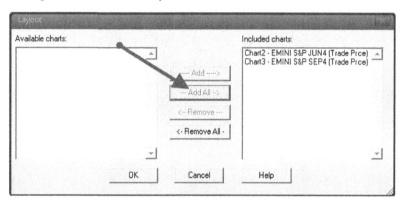

Add both charts into the layout and then choose OK.

8. Finally you need to save the layout by going to File | Save As | Type: Layout.

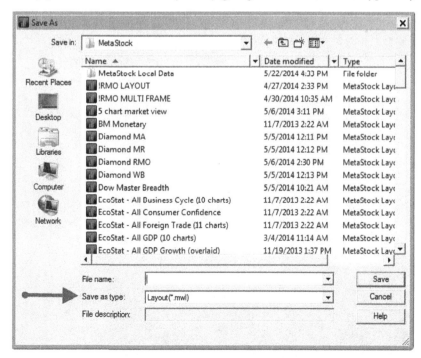

9. Select a file name and choose Save.

10. To open a layout, go to File | Open. Change file type to Layout.

Choose the file name you gave the product and choose Open. Your layout is now open.

11. Repeat these steps for each of the four templates to create your workflow like Dick Diamond.

A trading legend, Dick Diamond has been trading for a living for over 40 years. He has expertise in trading OEX options, S&P/Nasdaq futures, and Dow/Amex/Nasdaq equities. He offers in-person trading courses through his web site, www.marketmentor.com. Diamond has an MBA from the University of Michigan with a bachelor of science degree in economics from the Wharton School of Business. He worked as a floor broker on the American Stock Exchange. He left the floor in 1965 and has been trading for a living ever since.

NOTE: Page references in *italics* refer to figures.

short trade (examples), 48, *48, 52,* 52–53, *57, 57*–58, 62, *62*
  21-day/55-day/89-day (example), *60,*60–61
moving average convergence-divergence (MACD), 9
  crossovers, defined, 34–35, *35*
  defined, 34
  divergences, defined, 35–37, *36*
  See also Bressert indicator; moving ribbons
moving averages
  decision process and, 118–122, *119*
  defined, 29–34, *31, 32, 33*
  template for, 128, *128*
moving ribbons, 65–79
  bearish divergence (example), *68,* 68–69
  bullish signal (example), 67, *67*
  decision process and, 118–122, *122*
  defined, 43–44, *44*
  80/20 trade (example), 73, *73*
  long trade (examples), 71, *71,* 76, *76, 77,*77–78
  short trade (examples), 70, *70,* 72, *72,* 74, *74,* 75, *75*
  template for, 127, *127*
  upward momentum (example), 66, *66*

O

opinion, recognizing opportunity *versus,* 23
options, inception of, 4
overbought, defined, 39
oversold, defined, 39

P

paper trading, advantage of, 10
patience, as principle of successful trading, 21–22
personal responsibility, for trading, 21
position scaling, 24
Prechter, Robert, 1
principles of successful trading, 17–27
  manage your trade account, 25–26
  market entry tactics, 24
  opinions are for pundits, not traders, 23
  play great defense, 22
  pull the trigger, 22–23

quiet confidence, 18–19
  reviewing, 27
  sell too soon, not too late, 19–21
  strictly follow technical data, 23–24
  take advantage of market conditions, 26–27
  take personal responsibility for your trading, 21
  track your results, 25
  trade within your capital, 17–18
  use defensive stops, 24–25
  wait for 80/20 trades, 21–22
professional development, Elliot Wave International for, 1
profit and loss (P&L), tracking, 25
"pulling the trigger," 22–23

Q

quiet confidence, as principle of successful trading, 18–19

R

responsibility, for trading, 21
results, tracking, 25
RMO oscillator, 9–10, 99–116
  bullish trade (examples), 103, *103,* 115, *115,* 116, *116*
  decision process and, 118–122, *121*
  defined, 9–10, 42–43, *43*
  80/20 short trade, *100,* 100–101
  80/20 trade (examples), 107, *107,* 108, *108*
  extended rally (example), *112,* 112–113
  long trade (example), *104,* 104–105
  oversold conditions (example), 106, *106*
  short trade (examples), 102, *102,* 109, 109–110, 111, *111,* 114, *114*
  template for, *127,*128

S

selling, timing of, 19–21
slope lines
  moving averages and, 30–31, 33
  stochastic momentum and, 40
  See also technical analysis

Join Dick Diamond at his Market Mentor Trading Course, and soak up as much of his hard-won trading knowledge as you can.

Here's just some of what you will learn:

1. How to recognize and act on Diamond's "**80/20 trades**."

2. The **important nuances** of trading stocks, options, and futures, including the best time of day to buy individual stocks and how to "trend play" with options.

3. How to practice emotional discipline and **get rid of bad the habits** that thwart your success.

4. Which **trading indicators** you should use, how to set them to maximize their utility, and which **four indicators** present the best opportunities when aligned.

5. Perhaps most important of all: When to play close to your vest vs. **when to take decisive action** when the market demands it.

You'll get a uniquely valuable trading course with Diamond and his star protégé, Roberto Hernandez—that also includes **LIVE** trading. Dick and Roberto will show you their prep work, system setup, and how they scan the market for 80/20 trades. If the market offers opportunities, they will make actual trades during the course. That's how confident Dick Diamond is in his trading method.

To learn more about Dick Diamond's next live or online trading course, please visit:

http://bit.ly/DickDiamondCourse

Printed in the United States
By Bookmasters